50 Thanksgivings
Waterloo's Hockey Holiday

Tim Harwood

Forward by Ryan Papa

Copyright © 2020 Tim Harwood
BTSCP Books – Waterloo, Iowa

All rights reserved.
ISBN: 978-0-578-76228-9

For the staff and coaches and players and fans who have been my Thanksgiving family for 15 years and counting.

Other Books About Waterloo Sports

Black Hawks Chronicle; Five Decades of Teams, Games, and Players
The Legion Team; Forgotten Hockey in Waterloo, 1927-1930
Ball Hawks; The Arrival and Departure of the NBA in Iowa

Visiting Thanksgiving Opponents

St. Paul Steers	1964
Rochester Mustangs	1966-1967, 1999
Kansas City Blades*	1969
Green Bay Bobcats	1970, 1972, 1976-1977, 1980
Milwaukee Admirals	1973-1975
Sioux City Musketeers	1978, 1992
Austin Mustangs	1979
Des Moines Buccaneers	1981-1984, 1987-1988
Dubuque Fighting Saints	1985
St. Paul Vulcans	1986
North Iowa Huskies	1989, 1993, 1997-1998
Wisconsin Capitols	1994
Cedar Rapids RoughRiders	2000-2019

*The Iowa Stars hosted the Kansas City Blades in 1969.

FORWARD
by Ryan Papa

My first Thanksgiving in Waterloo is a game I will remember for the rest of my life.

I had already played a few prior games in 2010 as a Black Hawks affiliate. Being in the United States Hockey League for the first time, I was trying to keep my game simple. I was 16, and some of these guys were 19-, 20-, 21-year-olds, so there was a good age and size-strength difference, but I never played scared due to my size. I kept it simple. That was my mentality when the coaches reached out about Thanksgiving: just use my skill and hard work to my advantage.

When I got there, I don't think I really realized the full scope of the Thanksgiving Day game, the history behind it, and how much it means to the city and the organization. I didn't realize that Cedar Rapids had one of the top teams in the league that year, either. They had more than a few good players and some NHL prospects on their team. Being so young, the less I knew, the better.

As a player, you look around the stadium, and it's sold out. The whole town shows up. The atmosphere is almost like a playoff game. It was close all the way, and we were tied at the end of the third period.

I remember being on the bench a couple minutes into overtime, and Coach Fuki [Shane Fukushima] called my name.

And I was thinking, "Really? You're putting me out there in overtime?"

Ryan Papa dodging Cedar Rapids' Matt Hansen. ©Stephanie Lyn Photography.

A second later, I was like, "Alright, I'll just roll with it and see what happens."

I wasn't on the ice very long before Vinnie Hinostroza gave me a nice pass as I was driving the net.

I got a shot off. Honestly, from what I remember, I think it was a pretty weak shot, but it left a rebound. I followed it up and ended up putting it away.

The next thing you know, I was being swarmed by the whole team.

Everybody was going crazy.

The fans were going nuts.

We made it to center ice, and we saluted the crowd, and then we all went down the tunnel. Someone told me I was one of the stars of the game, so I got to come back out. Where I had been playing, we didn't have big crowds or do promotions, so it was my first time throwing a t-shirt into the stands…being 16-years-old and doing that, it was a pretty crazy thing.

One thing I remember vividly was all my teammates back home in Chicago. The texts started coming in. They'd never been to Waterloo; some of them probably didn't even know where it is, but they knew it was a big game.

"Overtime winner? Are you kidding me?" Comments like that buzzed in all night. It was pretty funny, but it was also great to get that support from my teammates back home and to see how happy they were for me.

When I came to Waterloo for the full season the next couple of years, rookies would ask about the crowds at Young Arena. I would tell them that nights like Thanksgiving and New Year's Eve are games that you're going to be feeding off the fans' energy the whole time. Your first shift out there, you're going to feel like you're flying 100 miles per hour. Just stay in it, get through those first five minute jitters, and get back to your game. They are days when it's easy to get up in the morning and go play. You want to win those games for the city and the organization.

Thanksgiving in Waterloo became part of our family tradition when I was a Black Hawk. Typically my family would go to my aunt's house for the holiday, but those couple of years, they all came out for the Thanksgiving Day game instead. I'd have 25-30 people at the game. They loved it. Later in the weekend, they'd go to Cedar Falls' Holiday Hoopla and see Santa Claus. They even adjusted to eating a pregame meal of pasta and chicken while everyone else is eating stuffing and mashed potatoes and gravy.

These games in Waterloo set the bar and made me say "this is where I want to be playing...in an atmosphere like this." When I picked St. Cloud State, I knew I wanted to play in front of fans that are as passionate as Waterloo Black Hawks fans. When I got there, it was with more of a sense of calm, being able to just play my game and not let the crowd impact how I played.

What I would tell a player coming into a situation like mine now is: cherish the moment.

I played four years of college hockey. I can't think of a time outside the NCAA Tournament or the playoffs that was similar. There are not many games that I've played in my life where you can feed off the crowd's energy like that. Not everyone has the chance to experience *any* games like that. I played for 20 years and only got to play in a few of those games, ever.

Don't take those games for granted.

INTRODUCTION

Coverage of Thanksgiving hockey in Waterloo has included almost every imaginable pun related to turkey, dressing, and other familiar elements of the holiday. The published wordplay appearing in the Friday sports sections the following day has included…

"The Waterloo Black Hawks served up a platterful of tasty scoring opportunities while barely taking a nibble for themselves…"

"Phil Osaer put North Iowa on a starvation diet to cap off a happy Thanksgiving…"

"…the Waterloo Black Hawks almost stood still for an 8-3 plucking…"

"…the timing couldn't have been better for the Waterloo Black Hawks to cook up a 14-3 basting of Des Moines…"

And this very involved lead by Doug Newhoff from 1986: "For days, the Black Hawks had been building an appetite for a heated battle with this season's arch-rival in the United States Hockey League – the Saint Paul Vulcans. Animosity was to be the main course."

From 1972 through 2019, the Hawks played on all but four Thanksgivings, almost assuring that sportswriter's leftover witticisms had little chance to spoil.

The first Thanksgiving game was hastily organized in 1964, but the holiday contest truly became established as a tradition in the 1970s and 80s. During some years when there was little going right for the team, the United States Hockey League, or Waterloo, playing on the holiday served as a reminder of happier times.

Other USHL clubs have experimented with their own Thanksgiving matchups, but they have given up quickly. The tradition is more difficult to establish in an atmosphere of expanding media and increasing distractions. Competition from other commitments – like the encroachment of Black Friday shopping into Thanksgiving proper – even dented Waterloo's holiday attendance for a time. Nonetheless, there is little indication that the Black Hawks won't take the ice in front of fans filled with turkey, pumpkin pie, and holiday spirit, as long as there is hockey being played anywhere in November.

Some fans may only make it to the Thanksgiving game during the course of a season, towed to the rink by more enthusiastic family members. Some come for the game as part of their broader homecoming associated with the holiday. Yet the family nature of the evening is more than gathering with cousins or uncles you might only see once a season. This collective tradition extends the idea of "family" to a much wider group of people: the crowd gathered around the rink – enthusiastic for warm-ups, standing in silent reflection before the National Anthem, or joyously throwing stuffed toys to the ice – is bigger than the capacity of any dining room table in the Cedar Valley.

Even if some of the extended relations are Cedar Rapids RoughRider fans, they are still welcome.

The other great virtue of the Thanksgiving atmosphere is the opportunity it provides to the 40 players who take the ice. Anticipation for the big crowd is passed from veteran to rookie each fall. Almost any player can produce a signature performance he will always remember. To do it on Thanksgiving is to save the memory in the collective hard drive of thousands; they may still be talking about it on Thanksgivings far into the future.

For each gilded moment by a future NHL or college star, the annual game has provided a similar chance for an eager newcomer, a stay-at-home defenseman, or a journeyman goalie. Many of those stories follow, providing a taste of Waterloo's holiday hockey ambience, regardless of whether the leaves have changed color or the crops have been hauled in. *Bon appétit*!

1964
Black Hawks 5, St. Paul Steers 2

Waterloo's Thanksgiving hockey tradition began accidentally because of a winter storm. The Black Hawks opened the 1964/65 season with three straight home games and were scheduled to visit the Green Bay Bobcats and St. Paul Steers during the final weekend of November. A forecast for poor weather led the Hawks and Steers to change their matchup from Sunday in St. Paul to Thanksgiving Thursday at Waterloo Auditorium (not yet renamed "McElroy Auditorium"). The revised schedule was announced on Tuesday morning, leaving only two days' notice for Waterloo fans.

Ticket prices were reduced to just a dollar for adults and 50 cents for kids under 12. All seats were available on a "general admission" basis. Under the circumstances, an impressive crowd of 2,878 made their way to the rink.

Those fans might have been hoping to see Bill Masterton make his first visit to Waterloo. The two-time All-American was with the Steers after a year away from the game. As a college senior in 1961, Masterton had led the University of Denver to the school's second consecutive NCAA national championship and was named Most Outstanding Player during the Frozen Four. Masterton signed with the Montreal Canadiens and eventually had a spectacular 1962/63 season with their American Hockey League farm club, the Cleveland Barons. When that remarkable year proved insufficient to bring him to Montreal in the fall of 1963, Masterton left professional hockey. Ultimately, his time in St. Paul later helped open a path to the NHL when the league expanded to add the Minnesota North Stars in 1967.

Although Masterton was back on the ice by 1964, he did not travel with the Steers for the Thanksgiving game. Instead of seeing the strapping six-footer skate for the visitors, Waterloo fans were amazed by the home team's 5-foot-6-inch winger Emery Ruelle.

Emery Ruelle was a contributor to Black Hawks wins in each of the first two Thanksgiving games.

At age 24, Ruelle was already spending his fourth hockey season in Iowa. He had first joined the Des Moines Oak Leafs in the fall of 1961 and played there two years. Ruelle moved to Waterloo for 1963/64, recording 21 goals and 34 points in just 28 games. He finished as the Hawks' fourth-highest scorer as the team won the USHL championship in their second season.

Just 2:01 into the Thanksgiving game, Ruelle intercepted a pass at center ice, moved into the offensive zone through the right circle, and scored the game's opening goal. It was the first of four that night for the native of Michigan's Upper Peninsula.

He scored again just past the midpoint of the first period; it was a quick redirection on a feed across the netmouth from player/coach Bud McRae. During the second period, St. Paul cut Waterloo's lead back to one goal twice; a Hawks score by Butch Leskun was wedged between a pair of Steers tallies and helped keep Waterloo in front. Then, Ruelle completed his hat trick thanks to a successful odd-man rush at 15:35, making it a 4-2 game. He added one more goal during a power play in the final minute before intermission.

Even through the third period did not include any additional scoring, there was a noteworthy moment. Hawks players were penalty killing in the St. Paul zone with seven minutes remaining when a scrum near the net almost turned into a line brawl. Ruelle, linemate Pat Casey, and defenseman Wayne Wirkkula were all sent to the penalty box with fighting majors. Steers forward Gerry Melnychuk and goalie Gaston Rheaume were given the same, and the two teams skated out the remaining minutes with short benches.

The win upped Waterloo's record to 2-2 and left St. Paul at 1-4. Both teams would improve, and the Thanksgiving result proved to be crucial in the long run. The Hawks finished the season 17-11 and earned their second consecutive league title, led by Ruelle's 24 goals and 39 points. St. Paul finished second at 15-11. Had the Thanksgiving game tilted the other way, the Steers would have been USHL champions with a better winning percentage.

St. Paul   0 2 0 – 2
Waterloo   2 3 0 – 5

First Period – 1, Waterloo, Emery Ruelle (unassisted), 2:01. 2, Waterloo, Ruelle (Bud McRae, Pat Casey), 14:32. Penalties – McRae, Wat (charging), 9:19; Guy LaFrance, StP (hooking), 12:16; John Rendall, StP (roughing), 13:55; Bernie Nielsen, Wat (roughing), 13:55.

Second Period – 3. St. Paul, Larry Alm (unassisted), 9:53. 4, Waterloo, Butch Leskun (Casey), 11:37. 5, St. Paul, LaFrance (Alm), 13:36. 6, Waterloo, Ruelle (Leskun, Casey), 15:35. 7, Waterloo, Ruelle (McRae), 19:26 (pp). Penalties – Wayne Meredith, StP (high sticking), 12:47; Mike White, Wat (high sticking), 12:47; Meredith, StP (high sticking), 16:21; Ruelle, Wat (high sticking), 16:21; LaFrance, StP (high sticking), 16:47; LaFrance, StP (misconduct), 16:47; Alm, StP (high sticking), 18:54.

Third Period – no scoring. Penalties – Duke Dutkowski, Wat (tripping), 11:34; Gerry Melnychuk, StP (fighting), 13:08; Gaston Rheaume, StP (fighting), 13:08; Ruelle, Wat (fighting), 13:08; Casey, Wat (fighting), 13:08; Wayne Wirkkula, Wat (fighting), 13:08; Dutkowski, Wat (tripping), 17:00; Dutkowski, Wat (game misconduct), 17:00.

Shots on goal – St. Paul 7-5-14 26. Waterloo 8-10-5 23.

Goalies – St. Paul, Rheaume (23-18); Waterloo, Jim Coyle (26-24).

Attendance – 2,878.

1966
Black Hawks 6, Rochester Mustangs 0

By late 1966, hostilities in Vietnam were escalating. The war was simultaneously far away and painfully close to those in the Cedar Valley. Notice of Private Russell Halley's death appeared in the *Waterloo Courier* on Thanksgiving Day. The Waterloo native had been killed three days earlier in a mortar attack. It had been less than two years since Halley had graduated from West High School, just more than a year after he had been married, and only two months since he had landed in the combat zone. At 20 years old, Halley was nearly the same age as the youngest members of the Black Hawks.

While the war became increasingly fierce in Southeast Asia, Waterloo prepared to celebrate the holiday season. City officials and business leaders agreed to light-heartedly rename the downtown streets to fit a Christmas theme: Park Avenue became "Santa Claus Boulevard," "Candy Cane Lane" replaced 5th Street, and Commercial Street was rechristened "Sugar Plum Lane" among nearly a dozen alterations. Christmas music and other comparable attractions were offered to enhance the atmosphere for downtown shoppers visiting the city's department and specialty stores. Santa Claus arrived by train on Thanksgiving evening, stopping first on the city's east side at 5:15, then on the west side an hour later to light Christmas trees in Lincoln and Washington Parks respectively.

After a holiday dinner and a stop to see Santa on either side of the Cedar River, hockey fans still had time to make it to McElroy Auditorium for a 7 o'clock faceoff against the Rochester Mustangs. More than 3,100 of them did. Waterloo had already faced their closest geographic rivals twice in the first month of the season; each club had won a close road game against the other during a home-and-home weekend which opened the Hawks' 1966/67 schedule.

With the transition to junior hockey, it's hard to imagine how any Waterloo goalie could match Jim Coyle's record five Thanksgiving wins.

On Thanksgiving night, the first period was penalty-free and evenly played. Both teams put seven shots on goal, and Waterloo's Doug Paul was the only one to hit the net, scoring a breakthrough goal with three minutes to go before intermission.

More than half of the second period passed with no change in the score, but then the Hawks pulled away with three goals in a four-and-a-half minute span. The flurry started when Paul Johnson deked to beat Mustangs goalie Tom Yurkovich with a backhander during a power play at 13:26. Chris Batley and Emery Ruelle followed up in quick succession. Two more tallies early in the third period set the eventual 6-0 final. Dave Mazur – in his first season with the Hawks – recorded the last goal to cap a three-point effort. Six different Black Hawks scored.

Goaltender Jim Coyle downplayed his perfect effort at the other end of the ice.

"It was the easiest shutout I've ever had," Coyle said after the game. "I honestly can't remember making a tough save tonight. The defense covered up very well…Rochester had a couple of good chances in the first period but fluffed them themselves."

Coyle finished with 17 saves in the shutout victory. It was the second of what would eventually add up to five Thanksgiving wins for the right-handed-catching former farm boy from Tillsonburg, Ontario.

Rochester   0 0 0 – 0
Waterloo   1 3 2 – 6

First Period – 1, Waterloo, Doug Paul (Dave Mazur, Dave Swick), 16:59. Penalties – None.

Second Period – 2, Waterloo, Paul Johnson (Bud McRae, Tim Taylor), 13:26 (pp). 3, Waterloo, Chris Batley (Jack Barzee, Mazur), 16:51. 4, Waterloo, Emery Ruelle (unassisted), 17:51. Penalties – Tom Yurkovich, Roc (high sticking), 3:08; Ruelle, Wat (high sticking), 3:08; Marv Jorde, Roc (hooking), 12:02.

Third Period – 5, Waterloo, McRae (Johnson), 3:24 (pp). 6, Waterloo, Mazur (unassisted), 3:38. Penalties – Bill Reichart, Roc (hooking), 1:58.

Shots on goal – Rochester 7-7-3 17. Waterloo 7-18-14 39.

Goalies – Rochester, Yurkovich (39-33); Waterloo, Jim Coyle (17-17)

Attendance – 3,115.

1967
Black Hawks 8, Rochester Mustangs 2

No player has ever come to Waterloo with a hockey resume like Paul Johnson. A starring member of the gold medal-winning 1960 U.S. Olympic team, Johnson was a world-class forward for most of a decade. He actually appeared in two Olympics, returning to the Winter Games in 1964. On three other occasions beginning in 1958, Johnson represented the U.S. during the IIHF World Championships.

"If Paulie was playing today, I'd love to be his agent, because he would be making a lot of money," noted friend and former teammate Herb Brooks long after both men had played their last game. "He was one of the most dynamic players I've ever been around. He was one of the top half-dozen American players of his time."

Arriving in Waterloo fulltime beginning in 1965/66, Johnson quickly became the Black Hawks' chief offensive weapon. Although he was 30 by Thanksgiving of 1967, Johnson was still near the top of his game and one of the finest players in the USHL. He proved that against the Mustangs, a team he had skated with when he was just out of high school during Rochester's 1956/57 championship season (at that time, the USHL was known as the U.S. Central Hockey League).

In the 1967 Thanksgiving game – like the prior year – one Black Hawks goal represented all of the scoring until the game was past its midpoint. Johnson was responsible for that relatively early offense at 10:33 of the first period.

Before he scored again late in the second, both teams lost a player. Mustangs forward Dick Haigh and Waterloo defenseman Bill Dobbyn were given match penalties for swinging away at each other with their sticks, sparking a bench-clearing incident near the McElroy penalty boxes.

The 1967 Thanksgiving game program cover featured many stars of the era, including Paul Johnson (middle left).

While the Hawks spent the latter part of the game with just a trio of defenseman due to Dobbyn's ejection, Rochester finished the night with a hobbled goalie. Tom Yurkovich hurt his leg, and Johnson, Jack Barzee, and the Black Hawks took advantage during the final 20 minutes. It was 3-1 when Barzee scored the first of his two third period goals at 5:51. The game was in-hand when Johnson put on a scoring exhibition in the late stages; in a three-minute window from 14:04 to 17:04, he recorded a natural hat trick. Added to his two prior tallies, Johnson finished his Thanksgiving performance with five total goals and an assist.

The 1967 Thanksgiving result was typical for the Black Hawks during their most dominant season of the era. It was one of 12 league games in which Waterloo scored seven or more goals, on the way to a 27-6-1 record and a fifth consecutive USHL championship. A dozen of those wins were recorded against the Mustangs, including a title-clinching victory in mid-February.

For Johnson, Thanksgiving was one of seven multigoal games in 1967/68. He would remain on the ice through the 1972/73 season. In 2001, he became the first Waterloo player inducted into the United States Hockey Hall of Fame. The following year, the Black Hawks retired his #11 jersey.

Rochester   0 0 2 – 2
Waterloo   1 1 6 – 8

First Period – 1, Waterloo, Paul Johnson (Bud McRae), 10:33. Penalties – Bill Reichart, Roc (hooking), 8:16; Pud Teal, Roc (tripping), 12:30.

Second Period – 2, Waterloo, Johnson (Chris Batley, Bernie Nielsen), 18:46. Penalties – Nielsen, Wat (interference), 4:58; Teal, Roc (tripping), 11:51; Dick Haigh, Roc (slashing), 12:15; Haigh, Roc (roughing), 12:15; Haigh, Roc (misconduct), 12:15; Haigh, Roc (match, attempt to injure), 12:15; Jim Smith, Wat (roughing), 12:15; Bill Dobbyn, Wat (match, attempt to injure), 12:15; Nielsen, Wat (tripping), 12:15.

Third Period – 3, Rochester, Ken Johannson (Marv Jorde, Reichart), :38. 4, Waterloo, Tim Taylor (Johnson), 4:51. 5, Waterloo, Jack Barzee (Dave Mazur), 5:51. 6, Rochester, Reichart (Jorde), 9:40 (pp). 7, Waterloo, Barzee (Keith Christiansen, Dave Swick), 10:26. 8, Waterloo, Johnson (Swick, Mazur), 14:04. 9, Waterloo, Johnson (Taylor), 16:35 (sh). 10, Waterloo, Johnson (unassisted), 17:04. Penalties – Taylor, Wat (tripping), 8:36; Swick, Wat (tripping), 14:59.

Shots on goal – Rochester 5-15-8 28. Waterloo 12-10-16 38.

Goalies – Rochester, Tom Yurkovich (38-30); Waterloo, Jim Coyle (28-26)

Attendance – 3,235.

1968
A Holiday on the Road

On the only occasion – to date – that the Black Hawks have ever played away from home on Thanksgiving, they were farther from Waterloo than they had ever been before. In 1968, the Hawks spent more than two weeks in Europe during late November and early December. They started with appearances in Switzerland and France, before playing a majority of their games in Sweden, then finishing in Finland. Taking the ice for 10 games in 17 days, Waterloo won twice, lost seven times, and earned a tie against opponents of varying quality. They met everything from national teams to local clubs.

After leaving from Minneapolis on November 21st, the Hawks' itinerary took them through a variety of major European cities: Geneva, Zurich, Copenhagen, Stockholm, Helsinki. The trip was almost entirely subsidized by the International Ice Hockey Federation. Huge, enthusiastic crowds came out to see the visiting American club, with attendance occasionally dwarfing the sizable turnout which Hawks players were accustomed to at McElroy Auditorium. Stops included two former Olympic hockey venues.

Some members of the traveling party already had hockey experience in Europe. Bud McRae spent time in London during the late 1950s, several years before coming to Waterloo. Paul Johnson, Bernie Nielsen, Emery Ruelle, and Tim Taylor had each traveled across the Atlantic earlier in the decade to skate for the U.S. National Team. In the years which would follow the trip, Jack Barzee and John Lesyshen went back to Switzerland and briefly joined club teams there between stints with the Black Hawks.

On November 28th – Thanksgiving in the United States – the Hawks lost 7-3 in Jonkoping to an opponent recorded only as "the Swedish Vikings." Few details of the game filtered back to fans in the Cedar Valley. Two days earlier, Waterloo had been shutout by the same opponent, 4-0. Later that weekend, the

Hawks picked up a 6-4 win against another team from Sweden in the northern city of Boden, thanks to four goals by Johnson and two from Ruelle. During the final week of the trip, the weary and injured Black Hawks were supplemented by a small group of Swedish players who helped bolster the lineup. Unfortunately, the reinforcements did not change the results.

After their international return flight landed in Chicago December 9th, the traveling party made a connection from O'Hare Airport to Waterloo and arrived in the overnight hours. The European expedition was not a competitive success, but it was a memorable experience. Those who participated had a chance to see the wider hockey-playing world at a time when the NHL and other North American leagues featured few European skaters.

1968 European Traveling Party

Butch Leskun (Head Coach)	Perry Goodsell (Trainer)
Bernie Nielsen	Bud McRae
Paul Sinclair	Wayne Wirkkula
Tim Taylor	Paul Johnson
Jim Smith	Jack Barzee
Emery Ruelle	John Lesyshen
Myles Gillard	Bill Matschke
Chris Batley	Dave Swick
Jim Coyle	Terry Hoath
Bob Keller	*John Kyle*
Fred Hagy	*Mike Lorenzen*
Joe Nutting	

Names in *italics* were members of the team's Board of Directors.

1969
Iowa Stars 5, Kansas City Blues 2

During Waterloo's USHL championship seasons in the 1960s, the Black Hawks encountered exhibition opponents from the Central Professional Hockey League with some regularity. From February 1964 through October 1966, Waterloo hosted five games against CPHL clubs from Cincinnati (twice), St. Louis, Minnesota, and Omaha. The visitors were top minor league affiliates for the Detroit Red Wings, Chicago Blackhawks, and New York Rangers. Due to NHL expansion, St. Louis and Minnesota had NHL franchises by 1967, and the growing hockey landscape provided opportunities which could not have been possible a few seasons earlier.

In the summer of 1969, the Minnesota North Stars relocated their Central Hockey League affiliate (the CPHL name had been shortened a year earlier) from Memphis to Waterloo. The new Iowa Stars were on the northeastern fringe of the league, joining teams from Omaha, Kansas City, Tulsa, Oklahoma City, Dallas, and Fort Worth. The 72-game regular season – the longest for any Waterloo team to date – began on October 11th. Entering their Thanksgiving tilt with the Kansas City Blues, the Stars were 9-7-3 and two points out of first place in the CHL.

Mike Chernoff delivered the top holiday performance against the Blues with two goals and two assists. Not quite a year earlier, the Saskatchewan native had made his first appearance with the North Stars; that single game would prove to be his only NHL stint during a nine-year professional career. Chernoff's season in Waterloo during 1969/70 was arguably his best in pro hockey. The 23-year-old led the Stars with 36 goals and tied his Thanksgiving night linemate, Bill Orban, with 75 points at season's end.

Already leading 1-0, Orban set up Chernoff's first goal from the edge of the crease 6:17 into the game. Then in the second period, Chernoff assisted on an

Orban power play goal which was the difference as the Stars took a 3-2 lead to the second intermission. The margin remained at one goal until just less than six minutes were left in the contest, when Chernoff flipped in his second goal of the night. His fourth point was recorded nearly four minutes later as he connected with Dick Redmond coming out of the penalty box. The defenseman and former North Stars first round draft pick took the pass and blasted a transition chance under the crossbar.

The Iowa Stars went on to finish second in the CHL regular season standings. The Stars were also runners-up for the league's playoff title, edged by the Omaha Knights in both circumstances. As for results off the ice, the Thanksgiving crowd of 3,519 was far larger than the average attendance at McElroy Auditorium. A financial loss for the North Stars – estimated to be at least $130,000 – outweighed the virtue of having their affiliate just a few hours away in northeast Iowa. Minnesota made a new affiliation agreement with the Cleveland Barons of the American Hockey League for 1970/71.

Iowa Stars goalie Fern Rivard had a unique Thanksgiving weekend, including this sprawling save.

Steve Willard / Waterloo-Cedar Falls Courier.

Although Waterloo's tenure in the CHL was short-lived, the quality of hockey talent that winter was unparalleled, as illustrated by goaltender Fern Rivard's experience over Thanksgiving weekend. During the Thursday night victory against Kansas City, Rivard made 24 saves for the win. Friday, he was recalled by the North Stars. Sunday – less than 72 hours after being in the crease at McElroy – Rivard was playing against the New York Rangers at Madison Square Garden. He made 39 saves for a 2-2 tie while dueling future Hall of Famer Eddie Giacomin in the opposing net.

Kansas City 0 2 0 – 2
Iowa 2 1 2 – 5

First Period – 1, Iowa, Walt McKechnie (unassisted), 4:39. 2, Iowa, Mike Chernoff (Bill Orban), 6:17. Penalties – Vic Teal, KC (tripping), 7:25; Rick Dudley, IA (slashing), 18:21; Dick Redmond, IA (elbowing), 19:13.

Second Period – 3, Kansas City, Ron Buchanan (Gary Veneruzzo, Camille Henry), 2:25. 4, Iowa, Orban (Grant Erickson, Chernoff), 11:01 (pp). 5, Kansas City, Norm Dennis (Don Giesebrecht), 18:48. Penalties – Gordon Kanneglesser, KC (tripping), 10:05.

Third Period – 6, Iowa, Chernoff (Danny Lawson, Marshall Johnston), 14:06. 7, Iowa, Redmond (Chernoff), 17:47. Penalties – Tommi Salmelainen, KC (holding), 10:35; Redmond, IA (elbowing), 15:42; Buchanan, KC (hooking), 15:51.

Shots on goal – Kansas City 10-7-9 26. Iowa 11-6-14 31.

Goalies – Kansas City, Gary Edwards (31-26); Iowa, Fern Rivard (26-24).

Attendance – 3,519.

1970
Black Hawks 6, Green Bay Bobcats 2

Santa Claus' arrival in Waterloo for Thanksgiving in 1970 was far more extravagant than it had been just a few years earlier. Instead of chugging in by train, the jolly old elf made his appearance via helicopter, following his earlier pattern of dropping in first at Lincoln Park on the city's east side, then Washington Park on the west side. The stunt was sponsored by seven dozen downtown businesses. Any of the historic animosity between east and west had been put aside – at least by the merchants on either bank of the Cedar – as they worked together to compete against the nearly-new Crossroads Mall at the southern edge of Waterloo.

Meanwhile, the Black Hawks had landed in the United States Hockey League once again to face mostly familiar competition. The Thunder Bay Twins were new to the USHL which Waterloo was rejoining. The Rochester Mustangs were absent for the first time in decades. The Marquette Iron Rangers and Sault Ste. Marie Canadians had both been on hand during the 1968/69 season and, of course, there were the Green Bay Bobcats, the only club remaining from when Waterloo had debuted in the USHL back in 1962/63.

Meeting Green Bay in a Thanksgiving game for the first time, the Hawks proved they could still compete with their longtime rivals from Wisconsin. Competing with Santa Claus was another matter. The 4 o'clock puck drop coincided exactly with Santa's appearance at Lincoln Park, doubtless helping to stifle ticket sales at 1,673.

Waterloo's Thanksgiving lineup included 10 players who had previously appeared in one of the earlier holiday home games. Additions to the veteran group included 31-year-old player/coach Wayne "Tuffy" Hall, a longtime pro hockey veteran with four NHL games to his credit a decade earlier as a New

York Ranger. Hall had visited McElroy Auditorium long before coming to coach the Black Hawks; he had been on the ice during exhibition appearances by the Minnesota Rangers and Omaha Knights in the mid-60s. In Waterloo for his first experience as a coach, Hall's squad opened the season 4-3-1 prior to the Thanksgiving matchup against the Bobcats.

WATERLOO BLACKHAWKS

No.	Name	Pos.
1	Terry Hoath	G
30	James Coyle	G
2	Keith Maiden	D
3	Bud McRae	D
4	Bernie Nielsen	D
5	Dave Mazur	D
6	Wayne Hall (Coach)	LW
7	Wayne Wirkkula	D
9	Jimmy Smith	RW
10	Jack Barzee	RW
11	Paul Johnson	LW
12	Chris Fennerty	RW
13	Rick Gignac	RW
14	Todd Lampman	C
15	Chris Batley	C
16	Miles Gillard	C
17	Bob O'Leary	LW
18	Terry Chrapko	RW
19	Dave Swick	C
20	John Lesyshen	LW

GREEN BAY BOBCATS

No.	Name	Position
1	Mickey Walsh	Goal
1	Jim Mattson	Goal
2	Jerry Frenette	Defense
3	Jim Jacobson	Defense
4	Bruce Riutta	Defense
5	John Mayasich	Defense
6	Carl Lackey	Defense
7	Emery Ruelle	Forward
8	Randy McArthur	Forward
9	John Harpell	Forward
10	John Gibbs	Forward
11	Matt Oreskovich	Forward
12	Bob Empie	Forward
14	Gordy Yewman	Defense
15	Jim Fuller	Forward
16	Paul Coppo	Forward
17	Jerry Lackey	Forward
18	Mike Funk	Forward

President — Jim Van Essen
General Manager — John Mayasich
Coach — Pete Buchmann
Trainers — Bob Van Lanen, Ben Schenkelberg

OFFICIALS	SHOTS				SAVES			
	1	2	3	TOTAL	1	2	3	TOTAL
Referee:								
Linesman:								
Linesman:								

The rosters for both teams playing in the 1970 Thanksgiving game (as they appeared in the program) included former Olympians Paul Johnson, John Mayasich, and Paul Coppo.

Green Bay scored first, just over two minutes into the game, putting the Hawks at a deficit for the first time ever during a Thanksgiving home game. Although Dave Swick tied the score briefly, the Bobcats went to intermission ahead 2-1.

John Lesyshen and Todd Lampman turned the matchup Waterloo's way during the second period, touching off a sequence of five unanswered goals.

The goal to make it 4-2 early in the third period actually proved costly. Defenseman Bernie Nielsen was playing despite being injured in a car accident a week earlier. As Nielsen slung a pass from near the half wall at 2:02, he was flattened by Green Bay's Fuzzy Frenette. The impact sent the veteran defenseman falling backwards, hitting his head on the ice. Paul Johnson scored on the play, yielding Nielsen's second assist of the game, although the

33-year-old was knocked out on the ice and never saw it. Despite the injuries, Nielsen would miss only a minimal number of games and finished the year among Waterloo's top defensive scorers.

Chris Finnerty converted a breakaway chance and Bob O'Leary added a final third period goal to finish Waterloo's convincing 6-2 victory. Jim Coyle made 30 saves, turning away all 19 Bobcat chances in the second and third periods.

Green Bay   2 0 0 – 2
Waterloo   1 2 3 – 6

First Period – 1, Green Bay, Bruce Werre (Paul Coppo, John Harpell), 2:02. 2, Waterloo, Dave Swick (Jim Smith, Bernie Nielsen), 12:23. 3, Green Bay, Matt Oreskovich (Mike Funk, Bob Empie), 15:46. Penalties – none.

Second Period – 4, Waterloo, John Lesyshen (Todd Lampman), 5:15. 5, Waterloo, Lampman (Jack Barzee, Chris Finnerty), 15:32. Penalties – Carl Lackey, GB (kneeing), 7:10; Bob O'Leary, Wat (cross checking), 10:02; Funk, GB (tripping), 11:42.

Third Period – 6, Waterloo, Paul Johnson (Nielsen, Swick), 2:02. 7, Waterloo, Finnerty (Barzee), 5:43. 8, Waterloo, O'Leary (Bud McRae), 13:02. Penalties – Fuzzy Frenette, GB (charging), 2:02.

Shots on goal – Green Bay 13-7-12 32. Waterloo 17-11-14 42.
Goalies – Green Bay, Bill Berglund (42-36); Waterloo, Jim Coyle (32-30)
Attendance – 1,673.

1972
Black Hawks 3, Green Bay Bobcats 3 (OT)

Retirements changed the look of the Black Hawks by 1972. The stable core of stalwarts which had been so steady through the championship years of the 1960s had dwindled to a half dozen players. Some of those veterans were skating only in diminished roles. After Wayne Hall's one season with the team, the Hawks had also transitioned from having a player/coach to being led from the bench. By the fall of 1972, Hal Schooley was Waterloo's third coach in three years.

Thanksgiving in 1972 proved notable in establishing the holiday as an annual event for the Black Hawks and their fans. From that fall through 1989, McElroy Auditorium would be open on the fourth Thursday in November for 18 consecutive years. Both the team and the community experienced dramatic and sometimes painful changes in that span.

Other USHL clubs were finding that the night before Thanksgiving could be a good occasion to draw a crowd. As a result, the Hawks visited Sioux City on the eve of the holiday. Waterloo dropped a 6-5 overtime game to the Musketeers, one of several additions to the league in 1972. It was just the second meeting between two organizations who would become fierce rivals later in the decade.

In Sioux City on Wednesday, new goaltender Steve Price made 45 saves – including eight in overtime – before the Musketeers scored the winning goal. Waterloo had forced the extra period after being behind 5-2 in the third. Despite the comeback, Schooley was dissatisfied that the Hawks had been so far behind. He scratched Paul Johnson from the Thanksgiving lineup, explaining that the longtime star had been on the ice for all but one of the Musketeers' goals the night before.

The holiday matchup was the first head-to-head game of the year between the Hawks and Green Bay Bobcats. Waterloo's Hal Murphy recorded the first goal late in the opening period. The 20-year-old from Southern Ontario had also found the net the previous night and would finish his first season with the Black Hawks as a 30-goal scorer. Larry Skime set up Murphy's goal, then made it 2-0 seven-and-a-half minutes into the second period. Another new addition in 1972, Skime had previously played for Green Bay, as well as representing the United States during the 1969 World Championships.

It was a 2-1 game going to the third period, but two minutes after the intermission, Emery Ruelle tied it for Green Bay, redirecting a shot moments after a five-on-three power play had become a one-man advantage. The former Waterloo leading scorer had been a Bobcat since the Black Hawks' hiatus in 1969. Waterloo took one final lead on Bryan Matlock's power play goal at 8:09, but Green Bay answered less than a minute later, leading Schooley to voice his frustration with Price after the game.

"There's the difference between a good goalie and a great one...a great goalie will stop all the easy shots. He went down to his knees too quickly. We are working on trying to get our goaltenders to stay on their feet."

Price turned aside everything else which came his way, finishing with 45 saves. That included eight overtime stops for the second consecutive night during a thrilling sequence of bonus hockey. Waterloo had an even-more impressive parade of chances during the ten-minute extra period; the Hawks fired 17 shots at Chuck Whalen for a Thanksgiving total of 56. Despite Schooley's criticism of Price, the 22-year-old Waterloo newcomer would go on to finish the year at 17-7-1, with a 4.11 goals-against average that was among the best in the league during that high-scoring season.

Besides finding work in the Black Hawks crease, Steve Price – like many of his teammates – also went to work during the day at a "regular" job in the community.

Green Bay   0 1 2 0 – 3
Waterloo   1 1 1 0 – 3

First Period – 1, Waterloo, Hal Murphy (Larry Skime, Dave Mazur), 15:15. Penalties – Cliff Purpur, GB (interference), 10:25; Russ Houston, Wat (charging), 15:37.

Second Period – 2, Waterloo, Skime (Mark Weinstein, Dale Pennock), 7:36 (pp). 3, Green Bay, Dick Purpur (John Gibbs, Carl Lackey), 14:00. Penalties – Lackey, GB (interference), 6:00; Garnet Currie, Wat (tripping), 10:53; Houston, Wat (hooking), 19:48.

Third Period – 4, Green Bay, Emery Ruelle (Lackey, Bruce Riutta), 2:00 (pp). 5, Waterloo, Bryan Matlock (Currie, Ken Selinger), 8:09 (pp). 6, Green Bay, Ed Chestolowski (Lackey), 8:45. Penalties – Mike Healey, Wat (hooking), :19; Pennock, Wat (fighting), 7:35; Bruce Werre, GB (fighting), 7:35; Steve Ross, GB (interference), 7:45; Lackey, GB (hooking), 14:55.

Overtime – no scoring. Penalties – none.

Shots on goal – Green Bay 15-9-16-8 48. Waterloo 17-12-10-17 56.

Goalies – Green Bay, Chuck Whalen (56-53); Waterloo, Steve Price (48-45).

Attendance – 2,530.

1973
Black Hawks 8, Milwaukee Admirals 2

Long before the Milwaukee Admirals became a top affiliate for National Hockey League teams, the organization was formed as the Milwaukee Wings in the winter of 1969/70. The independent senior club did not play in a league during their first several seasons. The team name was changed to "Admirals," when an owner – who also operated an appliance store – reportedly wanted to draw attention to a popular brand of refrigerators. The Admirals played most of their games in the community rink at Wilson Park on the city's south side, but occasionally took the ice at 10,000-seat Milwaukee Arena. Joining the expanding USHL for 1973/74, the Admirals would soon move all their games to the bigger venue; they graduated to the International Hockey League before the end of the decade.

Waterloo's Thanksgiving game in 1973 was the first of three consecutive times the Black Hawks hosted the Admirals for the holiday. It was also the first-ever meeting between the teams. Milwaukee ran into a Waterloo squad playing well on home ice; the Hawks were already 4-0-0 at McElroy Auditorium. They also – at least on Thanksgiving night – were the most dangerous penalty-killing team anywhere.

The Hawks and Admirals were already tied 1-1 less than five minutes into the first period when Ron Nagurski was called for crosschecking. Less than 30 seconds into the resulting Admirals' power play, Waterloo's John Lesyshen promptly broke the tie with a shorthanded breakaway goal set up by Jack Barzee. Late in the period, Milwaukee didn't even have an opportunity to touch the puck at the start of a new advantage; Barzee flew up the ice to score seven seconds into another minor on Nagurski. During the same penalty, Waterloo struck for their third shorthanded goal of the period when Dale Pennock redirected a Barzee shot.

The Milwaukee Admirals were regular Thanksgiving visitors in Waterloo from 1973 to 1975.

Barzee had been away from Waterloo for most of the previous season, playing and coaching in Switzerland. It was one of just two winters since 1965 that the Connecticut native had played for any team besides the Black Hawks. By 1973, Barzee's role with the organization had changed. Besides taking the ice for the team, he was president and public relations director for Black Hawk Enterprises. The company was formed in the offseason by a group of local shareholders; the Black Hawks had been operated previously as a community non-profit organization. In Barzee's multifaceted role, the Thanksgiving crowd at 3,272 was just as gratifying as his impressive first period.

The teams exchanged second period scores, putting the Hawks ahead 5-2 going to the third. New defenseman Charlie Brown built the lead at 1:15 of the final frame.

While all of Waterloo's players had to adjust their holiday plans to accommodate the Thanksgiving game, no one left home earlier than Brown. The 26-year-old commuted from Bloomington, Minnesota, in order to skate with the Black Hawks. His rigorous travel schedule was certainly worthwhile from Waterloo's perspective. Brown had won three college NAIA national championships at Bemidji State, represented the nation at three IIHF World Championships, and claimed a silver medal with the U.S. team during the 1972 Olympics. He would be named the USHL's Defenseman of the Year at the end of the 1973/74 season.

Barzee and Brown each scored again later in the third period. Appropriately, both goals were shorthanded. The Admirals' six power plays provided the visitors with one goal, while leading to five against. Two nights later, the Black Hawks rolled to another six-goal win against the Admirals, 9-3, in front of over 8,500 fans during a rematch at Milwaukee Arena.

Milwaukee   1 1 0 – 2
Waterloo   4 1 3 – 8

First Period – 1, Waterloo, Hal Murphy (Bob Lamoureux, Jim Gospodar), 1:42. 2, Milwaukee, Phil Uihlein (Rich Robbins), 2:53. 3, Waterloo, John Lesyshen (Jack Barzee, Dan Bosher), 4:43 (sh). 4, Waterloo, Barzee (Lesyshen), 17:30 (sh). 5, Waterloo, Dale Pennock (Barzee), 18:35 (sh). Penalties – Ron Nagurski, Wat (cross checking), 4:17; Lou Caputo, Mil (tripping), 8:29; Nick Lasch, Mil (high sticking), 9:39; Mike O'Hearn, Mil (fighting), 11:38; Lamoureux, Wat (fighting), 11:38; Nagurski, Wat (interference), 17:23.

Second Period – 6, Milwaukee, Phil Wittliff (John Womack, Wayne Caufield), 15:41 (pp). 7, Waterloo, Nagurski (Ken Selinger, Cliff Hendrickson), 16:36. Penalties – Lasch, Mil (fighting), 4:22; Hendrickson, Wat (fighting), 4:22; John Anderson, Mil (tripping), 9:04; Lesyshen, Wat (hooking), 14:47.

Third Period – 8, Waterloo, Charlie Brown (Dave Mazur), 1:15. 9, Waterloo, Barzee (unassisted), 10:05 (sh). 10, Waterloo, Brown (Pennock), 18:03 (sh). Penalties – Brown, Wat (hooking), 8:40; Jim Smith, Wat (hooking), 16:47.

Shots on goal – Milwaukee 13-12-10 35. Waterloo 15-16-17 48.
Goalies – Milwaukee, Anderson (48-40); Waterloo, Jim Coyle (35-33).
Attendance – 3,272.

1974
Black Hawks 5, Milwaukee Admirals 3

The atmosphere for the 1974 Thanksgiving game at McElroy Auditorium was a little different than in earlier years. It didn't have anything to do with the Black Hawks on the ice, nor the visiting Milwaukee Admirals. The change involved the 2,778 fans and their viewing experience. The Hawks had taken steps to clear the air, literally, as Jack Barzee described in a note to supporters earlier that fall.

"In consideration of the people who don't smoke and the participants in the game, the Board of Directors of Black Hawk Enterprises, Inc. have passed a resolution that there will be no smoking in the arena. You may smoke in the outer lobby and the restaurant area under the north side seats. The ushers will ask you to put out your cigarette and if you fail to do so, you will be asked to leave."

By Thanksgiving, most fans had adjusted to the new rules. They arrived for the holiday game to see a team experiencing a seesaw start. Waterloo had opened the schedule 1-4-1 before winning five straight games. A road loss in their most recent matchup left the Hawks 6-5-1; Milwaukee entered the game at 3-6-0. The scoreless first period was uninspiring.

"The basic Black Hawk shortcoming was the failure to play the physical, position-oriented style of hockey usually used when they are winning," wrote Jim Fickess covering the game in the *Waterloo Courier*. "Waterloo's checking was especially anemic in the scoreless opening stanza."

Line juggling by Coach Dave Swick started to light a fire under the Hawks by the middle of the second period. Defenseman Phil Iwaskiewicz blasted in a power play goal, followed by John Lesyshen's rebound put-back five minutes later. However, Waterloo squandered the lead before the period was over, and the game was tied 2-2 at the second intermission.

Bill Bennett's stature was unique when he came to Waterloo in 1974. His size helped him reach the National Hockey League a few years later.

Only 7:36 remained when Lesyshen – the Hawks' leading scorer from the previous season and an assistant principal at Edison Junior High – put the Hawks ahead with his second goal of the game. Subsequent scores by Paul Wormith and Bill Bennett extended the margin to 5-2 before the Admirals recorded a late goal.

Bennett's goal was one of four he would record in 34 games with the team. The 21-year-old had hoped to spend the winter with the Des Moines Capitols of the International Hockey League, but instead joined Waterloo in early November. At 6-feet-6-inches tall and 230 pounds, Bennett was described as the biggest player in the USHL, and there is nothing to suggest that was not accurate. The Rhode Island native was part of a large, hockey-rich family. That season, his brother, Curt, was starring for the Atlanta Flames, while another brother, Harvey Jr., had made his NHL debut for the Pittsburgh Penguins a month earlier. Bennett's father, Harvey Sr., had a long professional career, including a stint with the Boston Bruins in the 1940s.

Bill Bennett spent just one year in Waterloo, then another in the USHL with the Central Wisconsin Flyers. His unique size and hockey pedigree led the Bruins to sign him. Seasons with the Columbus Owls in the IHL and the Rochester Americans in the American Hockey League put Bennett in position to join Boston in the winter of 1978/79. On December 12, 1978, Bennett made his first NHL appearance, scoring the first goal of the night during the Bruins' 7-3 win against the Vancouver Canucks. He would go on to play in six more NHL games that season and 24 the next year with the Hartford Whalers, becoming the first player to appear for Waterloo before later reaching the NHL.

Milwaukee   0 2 1 – 3
Waterloo   0 2 3 – 5

First Period – no scoring. Penalties – Phil Wittliff, Mil (hooking), 1:03; Dale Pennock, Wat (tripping), 6:53; Pennock, Wat (slashing), 10:33; Ron Deval, Mil (tripping), 14:46.

Second Period – 1, Waterloo, Phil Iwaskiewicz (Mike Randolph), 8:22 (pp). 2, Waterloo, John Lesyshen (Randolph, Jim Smith), 13:35. 3, Milwaukee, Wayne Caufield (Bob Thomerson, Wittliff), 15:59. 4, Milwaukee, Deval (Mike Tardani, Ed Boucha), 18:59. Penalties – George Klasons, Wat (cross checking), 3:42; Boucha, Mil (tripping), 4:37; Jim Gospodar, Wat (high sticking), 4:58; Mike Mallinger, Mil (hooking), 7:13; Boucha, Mil (cross checking), 9:37; Jack Barzee, Wat (tripping), 19:20; Mallinger, Mil (tripping), 19:56.

Third Period – 5, Waterloo, Lesyshen (Ken Selinger, Bryan Matlock), 12:24. 6, Waterloo, Paul Wormith (unassisted), 17:49. 7, Waterloo, Bill Bennett (Charlie Brown, Ed Starkey), 18:34. 8, Milwaukee, Bruce Saulnier (Bill Frerrotte, Thomerson), 19:38 (sh). Penalties – Starkey, Wat (slashing), 3:54; Starkey, Wat (roughing), 3:54; Frerrotte, Mil (hooking) 3:54; Iwaskiewicz, Wat (misconduct) 17:19; Mallinger, Mil (cross checking), 18:51.

Shots on goal – Milwaukee 10-10-9 29. Waterloo 11-14-18 43.

Goalies – Milwaukee, John Anderson (43-38); Waterloo, Bud Heaney (29-26).

Attendance – 2,778.

1975
Black Hawks 7, Milwaukee Admirals 4

A snowstorm wrapped up in the early hours of Thanksgiving morning. The winter weather mostly missed Waterloo; less than an inch of accumulation was measured in the Cedar Valley while other areas of the state received more than six inches. Travel in parts of central and southern Iowa was difficult that Thanksgiving, with hundreds of accidents reported.

Even if Waterloo had been in the crosshairs of the storm, it would not have been the biggest concern for Black Hawk Enterprises on Thanksgiving morning. On the eve the Hawks' game against the Milwaukee Admirals, the Calumet, Michigan-based Copper Country Chiefs went out of business. The Chiefs had considered dropping out of the league over the summer. Average attendance of approximately 500 fans per game in the early weeks of the season convinced the club to fold. USHL officials planned to meet in Green Bay to reorganize the schedule for the remaining seven teams, even while questions loomed about the business viability of three other organizations. The Central Wisconsin Flyers, the Marquette Iron Rangers, and the Admirals were all reportedly in precarious circumstances.

Waterloo's financial position was somewhat better, even if the team's early record was poor. After making consecutive appearances in the league's championship series, the Hawks had started 1975/76 with a 3-8-0 record. The roster had changed substantially: Jim Gospodar and Ed Starkey were the only Waterloo players who had been on the ice for the 1974 Thanksgiving game and then also skated in the rematch 364 days later. Meanwhile, Milwaukee had won nine of their first 11 games and came to McElroy Auditorium with the USHL Southern Division lead.

Hawks defenseman Tim Anderson had spent more time in Waterloo than many of his teammates. Anderson joined the Black Hawks in January of 1975 after opening the previous season with Central Wisconsin. The 23-year-old had played junior hockey for Herb Brooks in the Twin Cities a year before Brooks became head coach at the University of Minnesota.

Tim Anderson is among the many Black Hawks defensemen who have made timely Thanksgiving contributions over the years.

During a power play 1:54 into the Thanksgiving game, Anderson gave the Hawks an early lead, hitting the net with a shot that came from above the faceoff circle. It was the first of two opening period goals for Anderson. Waterloo also converted another power play and went to intermission on top of Milwaukee 4-1.

"Tim scored a couple of beautiful goals, that's for sure," said Coach Dave Swick. "The first period was our best period this year...We took the game to them."

After a scary moment in the second, the smooth start became bumpy. Admirals veteran defenseman Lou Caputo took a puck to the face shortly after intermission. The eye injury which resulted had to be treated at the hospital. Caputo's teammates responded by putting 18 shots on net in the period, closing to within 5-3 by intermission.

Starkey broke the Admirals' momentum by adding to the Waterloo lead 2:27 into the third. Later, Anderson added his second assist and fourth point of the game, helping to set up a score by Jacques Rodrigue.

The USHL finished the 1975/76 season without any other club failures. Waterloo overtook Milwaukee in the standings and ended the year second in the Southern Division, just three points behind Sioux City. Yet it was the

Admirals who celebrated when the final horn sounded. Although Milwaukee's financial circumstances forced league officials to step in and operate the club, the Admirals won playoff series against the Sioux City Musketeers, the Traverse City Bays, and the Green Bay Bobcats to earn their only USHL championship.

Milwaukee   1 2 1 – 4
Waterloo   4 1 2 – 7

First Period – 1, Waterloo, Tim Anderson (Doug Falls, Jacques Rodrigue), 1:54 (pp). 2, Waterloo, Hobie Taylor (Marc Tessier, Dave Mathewson), 11:56. 3, Milwaukee, Lou Caputo (Bruce Salnier, Phil Wittliff), 13:31. 4, Waterloo, Anderson (Rodrigue, Tessier), 14:13. 5, Waterloo, Falls (Anderson, Rick Cabalka), 15:30 (pp). Penalties – Caputo, Mil (holding), 1:04; Mathewson, Wat (tripping), 5:34; Rene Daze, Mil (high sticking), 13:11; Cabalka, Wat (interference), 13:11; Rob Mackness, Mil (tripping), 15:25.

Second Period – 6, Waterloo, Jim Gospodar (Mike Phippen, Cabalka), 4:38. 7, Milwaukee, Wittliff (Gaetan Legault, Pierre Quintal), 10:52. 8, Milwaukee, Quintal (Mike Mallinger, Dan Lecours), 15:59 (pp). Penalties – Dan Dillon, Wat (slashing), 14:53; Mallinger, Mil (charging), 18:42.

Third Period – 9, Waterloo, Ed Starkey (Stan Blom), 2:27. 10, Waterloo, Rodrigue (Anderson, Taylor), 5:15. 11, Milwaukee, Jean Trottier (Lecours, Wayne Caufield), 14:37 (pp). Penalties – Mathewson, Wat (tripping), 14:14.

Shots on goal – Milwaukee 12-18-8 38. Waterloo 16-10-14 40.

Goalies – Milwaukee, Joe Bertagna (40-33); Waterloo, Gordie Woolnough (38-34).

Attendance – 2,021.

1976
Green Bay Bobcats 7, Black Hawks 2

For a vast number of Americans, Thanksgiving is likely to conjure thoughts of football as much as turkey and dressing. Waterloo sports fans could be forgiven if football overshadowed hockey on Thanksgiving in 1976. The game of interest did not involve an NFL or college team. Five days earlier, Columbus Catholic High School had defeated Emmetsburg 13-7 to win the city's first state championship. The 3A title for the Sailors came just five years after Iowa had initiated a playoff structure for the state's top football teams. The Columbus win was even sweeter because the game was played just a few miles away in Cedar Falls; 1976 was the first year that football championship games were hosted in the new UNI-Dome at the University of Northern Iowa.

Meanwhile, the Black Hawks were struggling through another difficult start. Waterloo opened the 1976/77 schedule 2-8-0. Five of their losses were by at least three goals. The tension was evident when the Hawks played a close game on the Sunday prior to the holiday. The Sioux City Musketeers edged Waterloo 5-4 in overtime, scoring the winning goal during a power play. Coach Dave Swick confronted referee Nick Argentine after the game and was saddled with a one-game suspension by the USHL. The league threatened to fine the Black Hawks $500 if there were any further incidents in the weeks which followed, and Swick had to watch the Thanksgiving contest from outside the glass.

Jack Barzee's first game coaching the Black Hawks began reasonably well. Serving as the Hawks' general manager by this time, Barzee was simultaneously trying to find players to make Waterloo more competitive. Two new Black Hawks were on the bench for the first time Thanksgiving night: defenseman John Albers and reserve goaltender Rod Manty. Waterloo had eight shots in the first period to Green Bay's 10, and the teams went to the dressing room with no score.

When the Bobcats broke through 3:58 into the second period, the Black Hawks collapsed. Just over six minutes later it was 5-1, with Waterloo's Kim King scratching out a power play score amid the maelstrom. Green Bay added another goal in the third before Stan Blom – playing through a back injury – scored the Hawks' final goal on an assist from the newcomer, Albers. Manty was in the crease for the third period, stopping 13 of 15 shots in relief of starter Phil Anchukaitis.

With Dave Swick (left) suspended, Jack Barzee (right) coached the Black Hawks for the first time on Thanksgiving.

The result was Waterloo's first official Thanksgiving loss. Making matters worse, the Hawks had been stopped on 10 of 11 power plays by the physical and aggressive Bobcats.

Swick was at least as frustrated from his seat as he might have been on the bench.

"We were scared. We didn't go into the corners all night. We were just plain afraid," he assessed, continuing, "And, we didn't hustle. We don't have the horses out there. They aren't my kind of hockey players…I don't think I can win with these guys. Maybe someone else can."

Swick did return, but the Black Hawks results did not improve in December. By early January, Barzee was back on the bench as Swick took a leave of absence. Barzee officially became the club's permanent head coach on January 21st, but Waterloo was unable to rally into the four-team playoffs in the now six-team USHL.

Green Bay   0 5 2 – 7
Waterloo   0 1 1 – 2

First Period – no scoring. Penalties – Bill McLeod, GB (high sticking), 3:37; McLeod, GB (high sticking), 5:49; Bob Falconer, GB (tripping), 7:11; Cam McGregor, Wat (boarding), 10:35; Ernie Dupont, GB (holding), 13:01.

Second Period – 1, Green Bay, Jim Carter (Terry Fyck, John Preville), 3:58. 2, Green Bay, Preville (Tom O'Brien, Dale Beerman), 5:56. 3, Green Bay, Bob Purpur (O'Brien, Fyck), n/a. 4, Waterloo, Kim King (Mike Farina, Dave Mathewson), 8:40 (pp). 5, Green Bay, Preville (Levi Byrd, Carter), 10:09. 6, Green Bay, O'Brien (Purpur, Beerman), 10:51. Penalties – Carter, GB (elbowing) 4:15; Corky Powers, Wat (elbowing), 5:15; Paul Pilon, GB (high sticking), 7:39; Dupont, GB (slashing), 13:33; Pilon, GB (slashing), 17:29; Mathewson, Wat (interference), 19:02.

Third Period – 7, Green Bay, Ron Pulak (Preville, Carter), 6:53. 8, Waterloo, Stan Blom (John Albers, Powers), 7:42. 9, Green Bay, Falconer (unassisted), 18:17. Penalties – Tony Hinschberger, GB (roughing), 3:29; Dave Klingbeil, Wat (tripping), 8:35; John Tweedle, Wat (roughing), 11:27; Purpur, GB (roughing), 11:27; Falconer, GB (high sticking), 12:42; Tom Machowski, Wat (high sticking), 12:42; Preville, GB (high sticking), 14:31; Falconer, GB (holding), 15:19.

Shots on goal – Green Bay 10-15-15 40. Waterloo 8-12-11 31.

Goalies – Green Bay, Dave LeGree (31-29); Waterloo, Phil Anchukaitis (25-20), Rod Manty (15-13).

Attendance – 2,191.

1977
Black Hawks 10, Green Bay Bobcats 6

From Thanksgiving in 1976 to the same holiday one year later, the United States Hockey League experienced the most fundamental change in its 30-year history. All of the USHL's teams were struggling to one degree or another, leading to a merger with the Midwest Junior Hockey League. The Black Hawks, Sioux City Musketeers, and Green Bay Bobcats came through the process and kept some of their senior players for the seasons which followed. The Austin Mavericks, Bloomington Junior Stars, and St. Paul Vulcans arrived from the MJHL with all-junior rosters. As a result, the Bobcats who visited McElroy Auditorium for the Thanksgiving game in 1977 included just five skaters from the year before; Waterloo had only four players on the ice for both games.

Less than a minute into the game, 20-year-old Roy Sommer scored the first goal, touching off a wild offensive evening and sending Waterloo on the way toward an ideal start.

"The guys knew they had to get to Green Bay early and they did," said Black Hawks Coach Jack Barzee. "There's such a parity in the league that any team can blow anybody else off the ice. And that [first period] was our best period of the season."

Waterloo native Ed Starkey added two additional goals during the opening 20 minutes. Starkey had made his first Black Hawks appearance in 1973 just months after graduating from Waterloo West High School. He worked as a truck driver, among other jobs, and went to college while also playing for the Black Hawks in his late teens and early 20s. During the 1975/76 season, the hard-hitting 5-foot-9-inch forward had been Waterloo's captain. Besides being a capable scorer, Starkey was always willing to drop his gloves when challenged, making him one of the most penalized players during each of his years with the Hawks.

The challenge Waterloo faced in this game came from a Green Bay scoring flurry midway through the second period. Two goals separated by just over four minutes nearly erased Waterloo's lead. At 13:28, Waterloo's Cam McGregor put the Hawks ahead 5-3, but just 11 seconds later the margin was back to one. Ultimately, Green Bay's rally broke down when Hawks forward Ken Yackel put the puck between the pipes twice within a ten-second span. Starkey then completed his hat trick with a back-breaking breakaway goal two seconds before the period was over, sending the Hawks to intermission ahead 8-4.

Both teams added two goals in the final frame, Waterloo made it 10-4 before Green Bay finished the third with the same deficit as when the period began.

Ed Starkey did not have imposing size, but his big hits helped opponents learn to look for him on the ice throughout the 1970s.

The unique hybrid of junior and senior players proved to be a good combination for the Black Hawks. Waterloo would go on to tie Sioux City for the USHL's best regular season record. During the playoffs, the Hawks defeated the Musketeers in a seven-game championship series, the first of two consecutive years Waterloo would collect the title against their in-state rivals. Through 2020 – after nearly 60 consecutive years of hockey in the Cedar Valley – it is the only time the team has won back-to-back postseason cups.

Sommer – who started the Thanksgiving scoring – wasn't there to celebrate the championship. Although he was nearly the right age to be among the Black Hawks' junior players, the 1977/78 season was Sommer's first year as a professional, and he was in Waterloo on loan from the Saginaw Gears of the

International Hockey League. The day after Thanksgiving, Saginaw recalled him. In January 1981 – following stops with several other teams in a few different leagues – Sommer had a brief stay in the National Hockey League with the Edmonton Oilers.

Green Bay   1 3 2 – 6
Waterloo   4 4 2 – 10

First Period – 1, Waterloo, Roy Sommer (Mark Veto, Tom Machowski), :27. 2, Waterloo, Ed Starkey (Cam McGregor, Reese Dobrick), 7:48. 3, Green Bay, Alain Myette (Dan Desjardins, Tom O'Brien), 11:29. 4, Waterloo, McGregor (Dave Annecchiarico, Dobrick), 14:07. 5, Waterloo, Starkey (Ken Yackel), 19:39. Penalties – Dave Mathewson, Wat (holding), 4:49; bench minor, Wat (too many men), 9:24.

Second Period – 6, Green Bay, Desjardins (Bob Purpur), 8:07. 7, Green Bay, Desjardins (Purpur, O'Brien), 12:17. 8, Waterloo, McGregor (unassisted), 13:28. 9, Green Bay, Myette (Jim Smith, John Preville), 13:39. 10, Waterloo, Yackel (Rick Clubbe), 14:01. 11, Waterloo, Yackel (Clubbe, Annecchiarico), 14:11. 12, Waterloo, Starkey (McGregor, Dobrick), 19:58. Penalties – none.

Third Period – 13, Waterloo, John Seidel (Scott Smith), 5:26. 14, Waterloo, Clubbe (Mathewson), 13:45 (sh). 15, Green Bay, Purpur (unassisted), 14:48 (pp). 16, Green Bay, Ray Richard (Preville, J. Smith), 17:01. Penalties – Desjardins, GB (hooking), :54; McGregor, Wat (tripping), 13:13; Yackel, Wat (holding), 17:39.

Shots on goal – Green Bay 10-11-12 33. Waterloo 15-18-14 47.

Goalies – Green Bay, J.M. Pominville (15-11), Gary Lyons (32-26); Waterloo, George McPhee (33-27).

Attendance – 1,704.

1978
Black Hawks 5, Sioux City Musketeers 4

For the first time on Thanksgiving, the Black Hawks' 1978 holiday game was a rematch against an opponent Waterloo had faced the night before. At Sioux City's Municipal Auditorium on Wednesday night, the Hawks had thrashed the Musketeers, 6-0. But their bus trip home was slowed by weather, keeping the team on the road until 6 a.m.

When the clubs met for the replay in Waterloo, they immediately took up their unfinished business. The Wednesday matchup had included 111 total penalty minutes, plus a pair of suspensions. The Thursday affair was just 33 seconds old when the Hawks' Stan Blom dropped his gloves with Muskies scoring star Walt Johnson. The next two minutes featured two more fights.

Waterloo was not yet at full strength when Sioux City's Brian Hartman scored the first goal, 7:30 into the opening period. The Hawks' Ron Milardo – who had been in one of the early fights – tied it almost nine minutes later. Milardo was one of Waterloo's junior-aged players, and so was Chuck Kessler, who scored the only goal during the second period, nudging the Hawks to the lead for the first time two-and-a-half minutes before intermission.

Blom and Dave Murphy of the Musketeers exchanged goals separated by just over a minute early in the third to put Waterloo's lead at 3-2. Then defenseman Tom Machowski gave the Hawks a renewed two-goal edge with under eight minutes to play.

The 1978 game marked Machowski's fourth Thanksgiving in Waterloo. The 6-foot-2-inch left-handed shooter had helped the Wisconsin Badgers win the NCAA championship as a sophomore in 1973. That same spring, Machowski was chosen in the seventh round of the NHL Draft; he was just the sixth American picked that year. Machowski was also selected during the rival World Hockey Association draft.

The Chicago native completed his Badger career and joined the Hawks for the 1975/76 season, but Machowski had hoped to continue skating for his college coach that winter. Bob Johnson was leading the 1976 U.S. Olympic Team to Innsbruck, Austria. Machowski appeared for Team USA several times during a pre-Olympic tour but was not chosen for the national team. Instead, he began a very successful stint in Waterloo, which included appearances in two United States Hockey League All-Star Games. He was also named the Hawks' Most Valuable Player in 1977/78.

Like Tim Taylor, Mike Randolph and several other Black Hawks in the 1960s and 70s, defenseman Tom Machowski found success in Waterloo after the disappointment of not making the U.S. Olympic Team.

Machowski's third period goal put Waterloo in position to extend a long home winning streak. Including exhibitions and the playoffs, the Hawks had not lost at McElroy Auditorium in ten-and-a-half months, since January 7th. The Musketeers had been the team which topped Waterloo in that far-removed matchup, and they made a run at doing it again before the Thanksgiving contest was over. Sioux City drew within one goal at 14:33. Seconds into the next shift, Machowski was called for tripping; before he was back on the ice, a Musketeer power play score tied the game.

Undeterred, the veteran defenseman – the second-oldest player on the Waterloo roster – fired in a dramatic game-winning goal. Blom (just three months older than Machowski) set up the play from behind the Sioux City net. Only 1:33 remained when Machowski sent Waterloo back to the lead and toward the team's 29th consecutive home win. The streak at McElroy would be maintained for exactly one calendar year, until the Musketeers defeated the Hawks 5-2 on January 7, 1979.

Sioux City   1 0 3 – 4
Waterloo   1 1 3 – 5

First Period – 1, Sioux City, Brian Hartman (Dave Pfannenstein, Kurt Dade), 7:30. 2, Waterloo, Ron Milardo (Brian Riley, Bill Kennedy), 16:26. Penalties – Stan Blom, Wat (fighting), :33; Walt Johnson, SC (fighting), :33; Peter Gillis, Wat (high sticking), 1:27; Gillis, Wat (fighting), 1:27; Matt King, SC (high sticking), 1:27; King, SC (fighting), 1:27; Dade, SC (high sticking), 2:04; Milardo, Wat (charging), 2:18; Milardo, Wat (fighting), 2:18; Mark Hallgren, SC (fighting), 2:18; Tom Hasenzahl, Wat (leaving the crease), 2:18; King, SC (holding), 12:52.

Second Period – 3, Waterloo, Chuck Kessler (Gillis, Blom), 17:31 (pp). Penalties – King, SC (tripping), 3:30; Dade, SC (high sticking), 5:30; Dade, SC (fighting), 5:30; Craig Brown, Wat (fighting), 5:30; Hartman, SC (roughing), 7:06; Hartman, SC (high sticking major), 7:06; Gillis, Wat (roughing double minor), 7:06; Mike Meadows, Wat (tripping), 7:18; Hasenzahl, Wat (slashing), 8:04; Dave LeGree, SC (interference), 14:01; Kennedy, WAT (interference), 14:01; Pfannenstein, SC (holding), 16:55.

Third Period – 4, Waterloo, Blom (Kennedy, Gillis), 5:04. 5, Sioux City, Dave Murphy (Johnson, Lance Breault), 6:15 (pp). 6, Waterloo, Tom Machowski (Don Jacobs, Hasenzahl), 12:12 (pp). 7, Sioux City, Dave Tracy (Johnson), 14:33. 8, Sioux City, Hallgren (Brian Gallagher, Hartman), 16:31 (pp). 9, Waterloo, Machowski (Kennedy, Blom), 18:27. Penalties – Jon Plummer, Wat (slashing), 1:45; Plummer, Wat (tripping), 6:10; Hartman, SC (tripping), 10:18; Machowski, Wat (tripping), 14:47; Tracy, SC (hooking), 18:42.

Shots on goal – Sioux City 13-9-11 33. Waterloo 17-13-15 45.

Goalies – Sioux City, LeGree (45-40); Waterloo, Hasenzahl (33-29).

Attendance – 2, 074.

1979
Black Hawks 5, Austin Mavericks 3

Four days before Thanksgiving, the Black Hawks played their first game in Dubuque. In a sense, Waterloo was the home team (or at least closer to home) for the technically neutral site game against the Hennepin Nordiques. The event was a benefit for Dubuque's youth hockey program. The teams skated at the 2,600-seat Five Flags Center, which had opened in March, and the Hawks prevailed, 7-4, in front of 650 fans.

The small crowd in the new facility was hardly a drop off from the size of the audiences attending Waterloo games at McElroy Auditorium. In a building twice as large, Hawks home games were attracting 1,000 to 1,100. After celebrating back-to-back championships during the transitional seasons from senior hockey, some Cedar Valley fans were staying home to express their disinterest in the first year with all-junior USHL rosters. The Thanksgiving game brought just 1,229 to the rink, the smallest number in Waterloo for the traditional contest up to that time.

Like the prior year, a long Wednesday game in Sioux City and a slow drive across the state left the Black Hawks poorly rested. The team bus rolled back into the Cedar Valley just as the sun was coming up Thanksgiving morning.

"Austin had to play last night, too," noted Coach Jack Barzee at the time, "so that equaled things out."

Balance between the two clubs was not immediate. The Mavericks jumped to a 2-0 lead less than five minutes after the puck dropped. Waterloo's Bill Grum was part of a small group of junior-aged players still eligible after playing for the Hawks a season earlier. Grum scored the first home goal at 6:38. Bob Motzko was among the newest Hawks; he tied the game by pushing in a backhander before intermission.

A native of Austin, Minnesota, Motzko had opened the season with the

Mavericks, then became a Black Hawk in early November. In high school, he had been a notable prep baseball player, as well as finding success on the ice and on the football field. Barzee was impressed by Motzko's hustle and desire to improve. In an ironic twist, Motzko – a future head coach of the Minnesota Gophers – was nicknamed "Badger" by his junior hockey teammates.

Days before Thanksgiving, the Hawks played a game in Dubuque at the Five Flags Center, a first step toward the club moving in the summer of 1980.

In the second period, Rod Krohn sent the Hawks to their first lead at 5:37. The Mavericks tied it almost ten minutes later, but then Krohn put Jeff Regan in position to cut to the net and sweep in a low chance which renewed Waterloo's lead just over two minutes before intermission. The Hawks were unable to build the margin until Regan's empty-netter with one second remaining in regulation, but the home side did carry play in the final 20 minutes, outshooting the Mavericks 13-7.

For the night, Waterloo native Greg Davis made 31 saves to earn the victory. Davis was one three local players on the ice (the others were Mike Murphy and Craig Brown), with the transition to junior-aged skaters offering the promise of more opportunity for locally-developed talent. The first all-junior Black Hawks team went on to win their division and reach the Clark Cup Championship Series.

Regardless, Waterloo's apathy toward junior hockey, coupled with Dubuque's relative enthusiasm (the Hawks played four more games in front of increasingly large audiences at the Five Flags Center in the winter of 1979/80), led to Barzee's departure. He took along the core of the 1980/81 Clark Cup Champion Dubuque Fighting Saints. Waterloo would not play for a league title again for more than two decades.

Austin   2 1 0 – 3
Waterloo   2 2 1 – 5

First Period – 1, Austin, Tom Erspamer (Bob Dore, Mitch Fossey), :39. 2, Austin, Dore (Erspamer, Scott Willman), 4:38 (pp). 3, Waterloo, Bill Grum (John Cook, Bill Grillo), 6:38. 4, Waterloo, Bob Motzko (Rod Krohn, Kevin Landau), 13:25. Penalties – Tom Sauerer, Wat (tripping), 4:04; Grillo, Wat (interference), 16:07; Darryl Finnel, Aus (hooking), 18:20; Kevin McCabe, Aus (slashing), 19:21; McCabe, Aus (high sticking), 19:21; Grillo, Wat (slashing), 19:21; Grillo, Wat (high sticking), 19:21.

Second Period – 5, Waterloo, Krohn (Tony Jerulle), 5:37. 6, Austin, Doug Tracy (unassisted), 16:13. 7, Waterloo, Jeff Regan (Krohn, Mike Murphy), 17:39. Penalties – Craig Ryan, Aus (delay of game), 5:37; Marc Nokelby, Aus (holding), 11:55.

Third Period – 8, Waterloo, Regan (Daryle Hanson), 19:59 (pp, en). Penalties – Alan Barth, Aus (interference), 3:00; McCabe, Aus (holding), 12:41; Landau, Wat (elbowing), 16:16; Tracy, Aus (interference), 18:37.

Shots on goal – Austin 15-12-7 34. Waterloo 13-12-13 38.

Goalies – Austin, Ryan (25-21), Scott Stoltzner (12-12); Waterloo, Greg Davis (34-30).

Attendance – 1,229.

1980
Green Bay Bobcats 5, Black Hawks 4

When Jack Barzee and the Hawks' veteran players left for Dubuque during the 1980 offseason, the "new" Black Hawks team which was assembled began with former members of the Hennepin Nordiques. Shortly after Hennepin had defeated Waterloo for the Clark Cup in March, the club was purchased by the Northeast Iowa Hockey Association and relocated to Waterloo to keep hockey alive in the community. Former Hawks goaltender George McPhee was hired to coach the team. A season-opening visit to the Five Flags Center illustrated a dramatic reversal of fortunes for the experienced skaters on each team: Bob Motzko scored four times as the Fighting Saints thrashed the Hawks 11-4.

Waterloo won just three times in the first 11 games of the season, but success during a pair of matchups with the Sioux City Musketeers was a source of optimism going into Thanksgiving.

"Things have been going a lot better in practice," said McPhee. "We're finally getting the frustration out and putting it together…Now we have a situation where we have to show everybody that we have turned the corner."

In an effort to bring "everybody" to McElroy Auditorium for the holiday game, the Hawks offered a special admission package: the whole household could attend for $10. With general admission tickets starting at $3.50 for adults and $2 for those under 18, the savings started to add up for families of four or more. However, it was not enough to push attendance (1,244) appreciably higher than it had been for the game a year earlier. Another factor which may have diverted attention from the Thanksgiving game with the Green Bay Bobcats was the fast-approaching first visit by the Fighting Saints, scheduled for Saturday during the holiday weekend.

Whether it was the impending game against Dubuque or the effects of an 8-5 win in Sioux City the night before, Waterloo had a poor start against Green

Bay. The Bobcats blitzed the Black Hawks for two goals in the first five minutes and made it a 3-0 game on Tim Lee's second goal of the evening at 12:41 of the first period. That tally came during a five-on-three power play while Jim Banaszek and Mike Murphy (the only returning Black Hawk from the prior year) sat idling in the penalty box. Back on the ice, Banaszek forced a turnover and scored during the ensuing shift, before Waterloo had come back to full strength. He recorded his second shorthanded breakaway goal of the game early in the second, and the rest of that period was played with a 3-2 score.

Waterloo was not able to solve future NHL goalie Bob Mason during five-on-five hockey, nor during their first five power plays. It was 4-2 in the closing minutes when the Hawks went to a sixth advantage; Todd Arrigoni scored from close range with 2:15 left.

However, Lee completed his hat trick into an empty net during the final minute. That proved to be the game-winner. Waterloo brought an extra attacker back to the ice and Arrigoni scored again with nine seconds to go.

Hopes of "turning the corner" gave way two days later. Dubuque upended Waterloo 17-3. McPhee left the bench in early December, replaced by another former Hawk, Ken Yackel. Eventually Frank Anzalone (who would lead Lake Superior State to an NCAA title later in the decade) took over to finish the season, with some improvement. In that year's round-robin playoff format, the Hawks came within one win of meeting the Fighting Saints in the Clark Cup Championship Series.

The ticket offer for the 1980 Thanksgiving game provided great value, but few fans took advantage.

Waterloo-Cedar Falls Courier.

Green Bay   3 0 2 – 5
Waterloo   1 1 2 – 4

First Period – 1, Green Bay, Chuck Lower (Dan Stankewitz, Tom Miller), 3:07. 2, Green Bay, Tim Lee (Ken Harpell), 4:38. 3, Green Bay, Lee (Bob Iverson), 12:41 (pp). 4, Waterloo, Jim Banaszek (unassisted), 13:35 (sh). Penalties – Banaszek, Wat (roughing), 11:06; Mike Murphy, Wat (tripping), 12:10.

Second Period – 5, Waterloo, Banaszek (unassisted), 1:11 (sh). Penalties – Murphy, Wat (slashing), :47; Scott Vanderboom, GB (elbowing), 8:33; Stankewitz, GB (holding), 9:51; Harpell, GB (holding), 10:39; Duane Holm, GB (roughing), 17:04; Holm, GB (fighting), 17:04; Chuck Gosselin, Wat (roughing), 17:04; Gosselin, Wat (fighting), 17:04.

Third Period – 6, Green Bay, Bob Ritzer (Lee), 8:06. 7, Waterloo, Todd Arrigoni (Mark Lescarbeau, Gosselin), 17:45 (pp). 8, Green Bay, Lee (Vanderboom), 19:05 (en). 9, Waterloo, Arrigoni (Lescarbeau), 19:51. Penalties – Jerry Thompson, Wat (slashing), 9:06; Lower, GB (elbowing), 11:56; Al Johnson, Wat (interference), 15:54; Holm, GB (tripping), 16:56.

Shots on goal – Green Bay 15-15-15 45. Waterloo 9-12-11 32.

Goalies – Green Bay, Bob Mason (32-28); Waterloo, Thompson (44-40).

Attendance – 1,244.

1981
Des Moines Buccaneers 2, Black Hawks 1

In 1980, the geographical balance of the United States Hockey League shifted to Iowa. The Black Hawks and Sioux City Musketeers had been part of the USHL prior to its merger with the Minnesota-oriented Midwest Junior Hockey League. The Dubuque Fighting Saints and Des Moines Buccaneers doubled the state's representation for 1980/81. Every season since then through the present day has featured at least four Iowa clubs in the league.

Hockey teams from Waterloo and Des Moines had skated against each other when the Black Hawks joined the USHL in 1962 and even before that when the cities competed on a less formal basis. Although the Des Moines Oak Leafs left the USHL for the International Hockey League shortly after the Hawks were founded, exhibition meetings were still a regular part of the schedule into the 1970s. That decade also saw increasing competition between the two communities at the youth and high school hockey levels. The arrival of the Buccaneers provided a rivalry which hardly required stoking, and beginning in 1981, Des Moines would become the Hawks' most prolific Thanksgiving opponent for the decade ahead.

In the last full week of November that year, the state's pride and attention was acutely focused on football, rather than hockey. The Iowa Hawkeyes had stunned the Big Ten, turning 1980's 4-7 finish into an 8-3 run during the 1981 schedule. A 36-7 win versus Michigan State on the Saturday before Thanksgiving clinched a trip to the Rose Bowl. With Christmas on the horizon just before the New Year's Day game against Washington, many of the state's football fans hoped to find a "giant" 26-inch color television under the tree, even if such a gift would have cost Santa a princely $1,000.

Throughout that winter and much of the 1980s, USHL results often looked similar to the finals of low-scoring football games. In the first nine matchups of 1981/82, Waterloo and respective opponents had combined goal totals which added to 10 or more each night. Over the full year, that threshold was ultimately reached 26 times during the Hawks' 48 scheduled contests.

The first Thanksgiving game between the Black Hawks and Bucs was a distinct exception. Des Moines' 2-1 win was the lowest-scoring game involving Waterloo all year, and one of only four Waterloo contests which featured fewer than seven total goals.

Despite a couple of first period Buccaneer power plays, the Hawks outshot Des Moines 12-7, and the opening 20 minutes was completed with no score. The ice tilted the Buccaneers' way when the teams changed ends for the second period, and near the end of another Des Moines power play, they broke through for the opening goal at the nine minute mark. Waterloo's Dennis Jiannaras stopped 14 other shots in the frame, and the Hawks put their netminder back on level terms moments later.

Just a dozen seconds after Des Moines scored, Waterloo swung from penalty kill to power play. During the opening shift of the advantage, Keith Hosken stuffed in the equalizer off a rebound. Although the Hawks had a couple of additional power plays before intermission, they couldn't break the tie. Instead, a hooking call at the 20 minute mark helped to settle the outcome. With defenseman Buddy Bender starting the third period in the penalty box, Greg LaDouceur put Des Moines back in front, setting the final score in the process.

Des Moines   0 1 1 – 2
Waterloo   0 1 0 – 1

First Period – no scoring. Penalties – Pat Johnston, Wat (boarding), 5:10; Jeff Strandell, DM (high sticking), 10:18; Mike Duffey, Wat (high sticking), 10:18; Bill Ries, DM (slashing), 12:35; Greg LaDouceur, DM (slashing), 12:45; Greg White, Wat (interference), 12:45; Johnston (slashing), 15:41.

Second Period – 1, Des Moines, Ries (unassisted), 9:00 (pp). 2, Waterloo, Keith Hosken (Chris Winters), 9:28 (pp). Penalties – Jeff Hanson, Wat (hooking), 7:19; Rick Swarbrick, DM (high sticking), 9:12; Bob Wright, DM (roughing), 9:52; Dave Wescott, Wat (unsportsmanlike conduct), 9:52; LaDouceur, DM (high sticking), 12:37; Kevin Tobin, DM (roughing), 13:24; Tobin, DM (misconduct), 13:24; Buddy Bender, Wat (hooking), 20:00.

Third Period – 3, Des Moines LaDouceur (unassisted), 1:04 (pp). Penalties – Karl Kringlen, DM (high sticking double minor), 7:44; Mike Messerer, Wat (high sticking double minor), 7:44; Bender, Wat (interference), 15:20.

Shots on goal – Des Moines 7-15-13 35. Waterloo 12-9-9 30.

Goalies – Des Moines, Frank Cataldo (30-29); Waterloo, Dennis Jiannaras (35-33).

Attendance – 1,218.

50 Thanksgivings

Many things changed between Thanksgiving in 1981 and the end of the 1981/82 season when this team photo was taken. That includes Co-Head Coaches Scott Murphy and Mike Brown. Players and staff with an asterisk were not involved in the Thanksgiving game.
Front row (left to right): Ernie Harker, John Spedding*, Buddy Bender, Dennis Jiannaras, Pat Baynes*, Mike Lanigan, Steve Naegle.
Middle row: Mike Messerer, Brent Hartman*, Todd Thompson*, Mike Duffey, Coach Scott Murphy*, Coach Mike Brown*, Rob Dowd*, Eric Wilman*, Jeff Hanson.
Back row: John Murphy, Doug Dietz*, Jim Banaszek, Dave Wescott.

1982
Des Moines Buccaneers 9, Black Hawks 6

One quarter of the 48-game USHL schedule had been played when the Black Hawks limped into Thanksgiving in 1982. Waterloo was just 1-11-0. Two losing seasons, plus an outlook which was even bleaker for 1982/83, were taking a toll. The Thanksgiving ticket count dipped to just 821.

"As players, we had to do a lot of bingos and fundraising stuff, which at the time I didn't really understand, but they were trying to keep us afloat and keep us where we could continue to play," remembered rookie forward George Griffiths years later.

Compounding the Black Hawks' problems for the holiday game, Griffiths was one of several skaters knocked out of the lineup by illness on Thanksgiving night. Forward John Murphy played a few early shifts but had to leave the ice with the flu.

The Buccaneers took a 1-0 lead less than three minutes after the opening faceoff when goalie Doug Timberlake couldn't snag a long shot, which found the net off his glove. Des Moines' Tom King added two more goals to make the score 3-0 before the teams took an early intermission. With 1:35 remaining in the period, a pane of glass broke, forcing a half-hour halt before play could resume. Waterloo's Dan Kimball followed up with a score after the extended timeout, but just seconds later, Des Moines was back ahead by three.

It was a familiar situation for co-Head Coaches Scott Murphy and Mike Brown.

"It seems like we get behind by three or four goals, then skate our butts off and get back in the game," said Murphy after it was over. "Then we say 'whew' and let up."

Waterloo did rally to tie the score in the second period, starting with a power play goal by defenseman Doug Dietz – a product of Waterloo's youth hockey program and a student at Waterloo West High School – at 1:33. Todd Christianson added another power play score seconds into Waterloo's next special teams situation a little more than a minute later. Then Captain Todd Thompson leveled the count. Des Moines responded by stacking up four consecutive goals – two before the second period ended and two more in the first half of the third – to push back to an 8-4 lead and take over permanently.

During the late minutes, Kimball and Christianson each scored for the second time, but the hole was too large. Des Moines' nine goals came on 43 shots, and play wrapped up well after 10 o'clock. Two nights later, the Buccaneers would win a rematch in central Iowa, 9-5. In fact, during 1982/83, Des Moines scored nine or more goals against the Black Hawks five times. Waterloo won just once during the ten-game regular season series.

1982 & 1983

HOCKEY SCHEDULE
UNITED STATES HOCKEY LEAGUE

Faithful hockey fans wondered if this would be the last Waterloo Black Hawks pocket schedule.

From the collection of Bob Batcheller; see more at thebatchellerpad.com.

The Hawks finished the season with a record of 6-42-0. The organization's survival was uncertain, because the club owed McElroy Auditorium thousands of dollars' worth of rent payments.

"It was surprising that a team that had that much history was in that much financial difficulty that they didn't know if they would have a team the next year," noted Griffiths, yet he and the Hawks would see another Thanksgiving in 1983.

Des Moines	4 2 3 – 9	
Waterloo	1 3 2 – 6	

First Period – 1, Des Moines, Scott Cross (John Demann, Bob McCorkie), 2:24. 2, Des Moines, Tom King (unassisted), 9:56 (sh). 3, Des Moines, King

(Greg LaDoucer, Dan Richards), 17:26. 4, Waterloo, Dan Kimball (Todd Christianson, Doug Dietz), 18:43. 5, Des Moines, Bob Anzalone (Greg Biskup, Dave Wallenstein), 18:54 (sh). Penalties – bench minor, DM (too many men), 3:30; Dietz, Wat (tripping), 4:53; Anzalone, DM (roughing), 9:29; Mike Duffey, Wat (slashing), 16:50; Jamie Husgen, DM (boarding), 18:25.

Second Period – 6, Waterloo, Dietz (Christianson, Kyle Parke), 1:33 (pp). 7, Waterloo, Christianson (Kimball, Todd Thompson), 2:51 (pp). 8, Waterloo, Thompson (Kimball, Jeff Hanson), 3:26. 9, Des Moines, Richards (LaDoucer, Steve Hammer), 11:20. 10, Des Moines, Hammer (Greg Shively, LaDoucer), 16:34 (pp). Penalties – Demann, DM (delay of game), :46; Duffey, Wat (delay of game), :46; Shively, DM (hooking), 1:22; King, DM (cross checking), 2:43; Demann, DM (tripping), 13:25; Carl Bryant, Wat (holding), 15:20; Anzalone, DM (unsportsmanlike conduct), 17:48; Demann, DM (high sticking), 19:16; Demann, DM (roughing), 19:16; Demann, DM (misconduct), 19:16; McCorkie, DM (high sticking), 19:16; McCorkie, DM (roughing), 19:16; Kimball, Wat (high sticking), 19:16; Kimball, Wat (roughing), 19:16; Duffey, Wat (roughing), 19:16.

Third Period – 11, Des Moines, Kevin Tobin (unassisted), 2:01. 12, Des Moines, Biskup (Anzalone, Tobin), 8:41. 13, Waterloo, Kimball, (Duffey, Hanson), 9:32. 14, Waterloo, Christianson (Kevin Noonan, Bryant), 17:19. 15, Des Moines, Anzalone (Wallenstein), 18:14 (en). Penalties – Hanson, Wat (holding), 3:04; LaDouccur, DM (high sticking), 6:25; Kimball, Wat (charging), 13:47; Kimball, Wat (fighting), 13:47; Kimball, Wat (game misconduct), 13:47; Hammer, DM (roughing), 13:47; Cross, DM (game misconduct), 13:47; Hanson, Wat (holding), 19:47.

Shots on goal – Des Moines 16-12-15 43. Waterloo 7-13-12 32.

Goalies – Des Moines, Mark Smorong (32-26); Waterloo, Doug Timberlake (42-34).

Attendance – 821.

1983
Des Moines Buccaneers 8, Black Hawks 7 (OT)

Waterloo's smallest recorded Thanksgiving crowd (770) saw a thrilling finish during the closing minutes and overtime, but they left McElroy Auditorium no happier for the late excitement. The matchup probably should never have stretched past the end of regulation; it was a game which slipped away from the Black Hawks in more than one sense.

Long before the first late November faceoff between the Hawks and Bucs, Waterloo had new life in the USHL because the team had been purchased by the Waterloo Warriors high school program. Keeping junior hockey alive would help assure that there would be ice for the city's high school and youth squads. New coach Harry Ray built a roster with several talented forwards who would improve the club's fortunes in the following years. The future stars included incomparable goal producer Rod Taylor – who would send 115 shots between the pipes during three seasons with the club – and Tom Bissett, who eventually played in the NHL for the Detroit Red Wings.

However, at the start of 1983/84, results on the ice were slow to improve. The Hawks were on a four-game losing streak and owned a 4-10-1 record by the time Thanksgiving arrived.

Waterloo led by one count or another from 6:02 of the first period until less than nine minutes remained in the third. Taylor scored the only goal of the first period. George Griffiths, Kevin Noonan, and Kent Middleton helped push the Hawks to their largest lead, 4-1, by 12:32 of a penalty-filled second period. By the time the teams went to the locker room at the second intermission, it was a 5-3 game, with six power play goals and one shorthanded score recorded during the middle frame.

By contrast, the third period did not include any penalties. The visitors scored three goals at even strength, swinging to the lead for the first time at

13:38. Undaunted, Waterloo went back in front before the end of regulation. The Hawks had recently acquired Dan Karabelinkoff from the Austin Mavericks, and with 2:20 to go, the newcomer leveled the score at 6-6. Then with eight seconds remaining, it looked like Taylor's second goal of the night would lift Waterloo to a win.

This promotional photo, dubbed "The Ice House Gang," features many members of the 1983/84 Black Hawks, including Kevin Noonan (left), Tom Bissett (third from the left), Rod Taylor (with guitar case), Mark Lanigan (behind Taylor's shoulder), George Griffiths (second from right), and Mark Pijanowski (right). Coach Harry Ray is kneeling in front. From the collection of George Griffiths.

Unfortunately, a faceoff in the Black Hawks' zone during the limited remaining time led to a controversial equalizer. Buccaneer center Steve Hammer kicked the puck from the dot toward the Waterloo net. It bounced, skipped, and slipped in. That questionable goal sent the teams to overtime. The Hawks had been unable to finish despite holding a large lead for a long time and a small (but seemingly timely) lead for a short time. The home club had one more chance to win it during the extra period, but Griffiths' bid for his second goal of the night on a breakaway was turned aside by Des Moines netminder Mark Smorong.

That stop delivered Smorong's second consecutive Thanksgiving victory moments later when Scott Cross flipped in the game-winner before the overtime had reached the one minute mark. Waterloo took the loss despite outshooting the Bucs 43-33. The Hawks' winless streak – extended to five by the Thanksgiving defeat – would eventually stretch to 12 games before a 13-4 victory against the Bloomington Jr. Stars on December 17th.

Des Moines   0 3 4 1 – 8
Waterloo   1 4 2 0 – 7

First Period – 1, Waterloo, Rod Taylor (unassisted), 6:02. Penalties – Greg Biskup, DM (slashing), 13:06.

Second Period – 2, Waterloo, George Griffiths (Paul McDonald), 1:28 (pp). 3, Des Moines, Tim Mishler (Dan Richards), 3:47 (pp). 4, Waterloo, Kevin Noonan (Tom Bissett, Doug Menzies), 8:40 (pp). 5, Waterloo, Kent Middleton (Cary Gilbert), 12:32 (sh). 6, Des Moines, Scott Purpur (Richards), 14:30 (pp). 7, Des Moines, Jeff Loser (Richards, Purpur), 17:09 (pp). 8, Waterloo, Noonan (McDonald), 19:49 (pp). Penalties – John Demann, DM (slashing), :11; T.C. Sullivan, Wat (holding), 2:37; Demann, DM (interference), 4:42; Mark Reinikka, DM (tripping), 7:50; Griffiths, Wat (roughing), 8:06; Steve Hammer, DM (roughing double minor), 8:06; Sullivan, Wat (holding), 11:56; Griffiths, Wat (roughing), 12:59; bench minor, Wat (too many men), 15:49; Demann, DM (hooking), 18:34.

Third Period – 9, Des Moines, Richards (Loser), 8:39. 10, Des Moines, Dan Dace (Rick Rice), 11:10. 11, Des Moines, Hammer (Richards), 12:38. 12, Waterloo, Dan Karabelinkoff (Bissett), 17:40. 13, Waterloo, Taylor (unassisted), 19:52. 14, Des Moines, Hammer (unassisted), 19:54. Penalties – none.

Overtime – 15, Des Moines, Scott Cross (Mishler), :54. Penalties – none.

Shots on goal – Des Moines 8-9-14-2 33. Waterloo 14-16-12-1 43.

Goalies – Des Moines, Mark Smorong (43-36); Waterloo, Jim Hatt (33-25).

Attendance – 770.

1984
Black Hawks 14, Des Moines Buccaneers 3

The early months of the 1984/85 schedule suggested a hockey renaissance had arrived in Waterloo after four brutal years. From the time the core of the 1979/80 Black Hawks had moved to Dubuque, Waterloo teams had not won more than 16 games in a season. During the fall of 1984, the Hawks opened with wins in five of their first six games. They earned their 10th win on the night before Thanksgiving, 9-6 in Des Moines. It was the 11th game in which the club had scored six goals or more. With a 10-7-0 record at the outset of a rematch against the Buccaneers, Waterloo was already in position to equal their win total from the full 1983/84 campaign.

Rod Taylor and Tom Bissett were shining. Taylor owned a league-high 24 goals. Bissett was setting up Taylor and his other teammates to the tune of 41 total points. Their offense was augmented by a pair of forwards from Waterloo's rival high school programs, who had played as either teammates or opponents since their earliest introduction to the game on frozen backyard rinks. Scott Dolan had starred for Columbus High School; a four-goal Thanksgiving eve performance in Des Moines pushed him up to 25 USHL points. Jim Tyler was a Waterloo Warriors product but had played his first USHL games for the Dubuque Fighting Saints before coming to the Black Hawks in the latter part of 1983/84. Tyler took the ice on Thanksgiving with 31 points, but added to that number quickly.

During the game's first power play, Taylor and Bissett set up Tyler at 4:44. Just seven seconds into a subsequent advantage, Tyler struck again at 7:18. He was denied a natural hat trick at 12:33 only because the Bucs had wedged a shorthanded goal in between. Nevertheless, the rout was on with a pair of goals by E.J. Sauer and a tally by George Griffiths before the game reached intermission, making the score 6-2.

Jim Tyler leaps after a goal against Des Moines.

Robin Scholz / Waterloo-Cedar Falls Courier.

After three assists in the opening 20 minutes, Taylor scored two goals in the first eight minutes of the second. All totaled, the Hawks had four in the period, extending their lead to 10-2. Taylor finished his hat trick 3:13 into the final frame. With two more goals for Griffiths in the last six minutes of regulation, the Hawks collectively had a hat trick of hat tricks: Tyler, Taylor, and Griffiths. The 14-3 finish was Waterloo's highest-scoring performance versus a league opponent since 1972.

Des Moines put 39 shots on net during the game, with just nine in the third (both relatively conservative numbers for the era). Coach Harry Ray glowed about the Hawks' defense more than anything after the game was over.

"That's what pleases me most about tonight's performance. Our team defensive play was much better than it has been," Ray said. "We've gotta play defense with the same enthusiasm we play offense."

Unfortunately, the Hawks were not a team built for defense. Waterloo lost their next five games after Thanksgiving. As the offense encountered more difficult times, the team went 1-7-0 between the win against Des Moines and Christmas. More difficulties beset the Hawks in January before a strong finish. Waterloo ended the year in the middle of the pack at 21-27-0 before being swept in a first round playoff series by the Dubuque Fighting Saints.

Des Moines   2 0 1 – 3
Waterloo   6 4 4 – 14

First Period – 1, Waterloo, Jim Tyler (Rod Taylor, Tom Bissett), 4:44 (pp). 2, Waterloo, Tyler (Bissett, Kirk Burris), 7:18 (pp). 3, Des Moines, Mark Pijanowski (unassisted), 10:33 (sh). 4, Waterloo, Tyler (unassisted), 12:23 (pp). 5, Waterloo, E.J. Sauer (Taylor, Quinn Sandness), 14:43. 6, Waterloo, George Griffiths (Steve Dettloff, Burris), 15:31. 7, Waterloo, Sauer (Taylor, Bissett), 18:29. 8, Des Moines, David Drown (Tim O'Neil, Tim Bottom), 18:37. Penalties – Rob Harris, DM (cross checking), 4:21; Myron Freund, DM (holding), 7:11; Steve Wiskow, DM (cross checking), 9:31; Harris, DM (cross checking), 10:49; Drown, DM (roughing), 15:59; Tyler, Wat (roughing), 15:59.

Second Period – 9, Waterloo, Taylor (Bissett), 1:18. 10, Waterloo, Scott Dolan (Tyler, John Bowkus), 3:18. 11, Waterloo, Taylor (Sauer, Bissett), 7:14. 12, Waterloo, Dettloff (Ray Kopitsch), 14:17. Penalties – Mark Harmes, Wat (slashing), 9:05; Dolan, Wat (slashing), 10:53.

Third Period – 13, Waterloo, Taylor (Bissett), 3:13 (pp). 14, Waterloo, Bissett (Tyler, Taylor), 5:45 (pp). 15, Waterloo, Griffiths (Bowkus, Doug Dietz), 14:27. 16, Waterloo, Griffiths (Dettloff), 18:19. 17, Des Moines, John Hart (Wiskow), 19:59 (pp). Penalties – Harris, DM (tripping), 2:49; Brad Nelson, DM (holding), 5:01; Sandness, Wat (elbowing), 6:19; Sandness, Wat (cross checking), 11:41; Harris, DM (high sticking), 12:01; Jeff Harper, Wat (holding), 12:01; Griffiths, Wat (high sticking), 18:39.

Shots on goal – Des Moines 15-15-9 39. Waterloo 27-18-16 61.

Goalies – Des Moines, Scott Olson & Don Johnson (61-47); Waterloo, Mike Williams (39-36).

Attendance – 880.

1985
Black Hawks 5, Dubuque Fighting Saints 4

During much of USHL history, the league had fewer than ten teams. Membership was at nine for the 1985/86 season. The 48-game schedule was unbalanced, and the Black Hawks faced some opponents as many as eight times that winter.

"There was a lot more animosity built up between players, and there was a lot more physicality in the average game," recalled goaltender Brett Klosowski.

Since 1980, there had been no opponent the Black Hawks and their fans wanted to beat more than the Dubuque Fighting Saints. Yet entering the fall of 1985, the Hawks had just five wins in 42 regular season meetings. Dubuque had also claimed all seven head-to-head playoff games, including a sweep the previous spring. New Coach Jeff Arf and an almost completely remade roster did not fare better when Waterloo visited Dubuque for the first time in the young season, losing 9-2 on November 10th.

Two-and-a-half weeks later, the Thanksgiving rematch began poorly. The Saints' starting line celebrated a goal when Kurt Kabat found the net just ten seconds after the opening faceoff. Although defenseman Chris Kleven leveled the score five minutes later, a flurry of goals late in the period favored the visitors. Dubuque outscored Waterloo 3-1 in the five minutes before intermission to take a 4-2 lead.

"I thought about coming in here [the locker room] and really tearing into them," Arf told the *Waterloo Courier* in postgame comments. "Their heads weren't in the game."

But Arf took a more moderate tone; that approach worked with the young club. In the first shift of the second period, leading scorer Chris Scheid recorded his 23rd goal of the season (it was only Waterloo's 18th game) at the

26-second mark. Then he tied it at 3:02. The Hawks' improvement didn't happen only in the offensive zone. After being outshot 25-9 in the first period, chances in the second were even at nine apiece.

The relatively quiet defensive frame was an unexpected respite for Klosowski, who was accustomed to seeing the puck quite a bit more on a typical night.

"Over the course of my two seasons in Waterloo, we allowed an average of 43 or 44 shots per game," Klosowski said, "That was the name of the game back then."

In 1985, the 5-foot-8-inch Klosowski was one of several players who had previously played Minnesota high school hockey before coming to Waterloo. The former Duluth East Greyhound established himself as Waterloo's regular netminder early in 1985/86. He was ultimately recruited to join Minnesota-Duluth as a freshman in 1987/88 but transferred to Wisconsin-Superior partway through that year and eventually helped the Yellowjackets reach the final weekend of the NCAA Division III hockey tournament.

Brett Klosowski provided the foundation the Black Hawks needed to win the only Thanksgiving game to date against the Dubuque Fighting Saints.

On Thanksgiving in 1985, Klosowski pulled the Hawks through a trying third period. The Saints outshot Waterloo 19-13 in the final 20 minutes but did not score. Instead, Waterloo was in the lead most of the way, thanks to Mike Notermann's goal at 3:39. After also hitting the net late in the first period, Notermann joined Scheid with a two-goal performance. Klosowski finished with 49 saves, the most by a Black Hawks goalie in a Thanksgiving game up to that time.

Waterloo ultimately won three of eight games against the Saints in 1985/86.

The following season, the Hawks would claim a head-to-head series versus Dubuque for the first time (taking four of seven contests), as well as eliminating the Fighting Saints from the 1987 playoffs during a five-game set.

Dubuque   4 0 0 – 4
Waterloo   2 2 1 – 5

First Period – 1, Dubuque, Kurt Kabat (Georg Thiele), :10. 2, Waterloo, Chris Kleven (Jeff Nevitt, Chris Scheid), 5:19. 3, Dubuque, Tim Breslin (Gerald Higgins), 15:09. 4, Dubuque, Arik Mathison (unassisted), 16:26. 5, Waterloo, Mike Notermann (Brian Cook), 18:50. 6, Dubuque, Bill Cody (Higgins, Gary Dixon), 19:17. Penalties – Chris Campbell, Wat (elbowing), 8:35.

Second Period – 7, Waterloo, Scheid (Nevitt), :26. 8, Waterloo, Scheid (Kleven), 3:02. Penalties – Jeff Swanson, Wat (slashing), 4:36; Kord Cernich, Dbq (hooking), 12:24; Kleven, Wat (elbowing), 18:59; Cernich, Dbq (high sticking), 20:00.

Third Period – 9, Waterloo, Notermann (Mike Finke, Swanson), 3:39. Penalties – Brian Kraft, Dbq (roughing), 3:45; Scott Allen, Wat (roughing), 3:45; Kleven, Wat (roughing) 13:09.

Shots on goal – Dubuque 25-9-19 53. Waterloo 9-9-13 31.

Goalies – Dubuque, Dave DePinto (31-26); Waterloo Brett Klosowski (53-49)

Attendance – 791.

1986
St. Paul Vulcans 7, Black Hawks 3

As the holidays approached in 1986, more than 3,500 Waterloo John Deere employees had been on strike for three months. The company-wide labor dispute had started in the overnight hours on August 23rd. UAW members wanted assurances that wages would keep pace with inflation and also sought improvements to Deere's pension structure. Meanwhile, company leaders were sizing up more than $100 million in operating losses from the early part of the year as American agriculture struggled through the decade's farm crisis. Negotiations had broken off near the end of the week before Thanksgiving. It was the second time during the strike that Deere and the union had walked away from talks when the two sides couldn't find enough common ground to continue discussions.

Work wouldn't resume until early February.

The Black Hawks and St. Paul Vulcans were involved in their own long-running dispute that autumn; Paul Daleiden was the wishbone both teams were pulling on. The defenseman had been captain of his Spring Lake Park High School team, and his rights belonged to the Black Hawks. However, Daleiden would have preferred to play for the Vulcans and attended St. Paul's training camp in September. Almost two months into the schedule, he was still off the ice in Minnesota, and the two teams remained unable to resolve their differences. Approaching the Thanksgiving contest – their first meeting of the season – Coach Jeff Arf anticipated that the animosity between the organizations had spread to the two rosters.

"It'll be a knock-em-down battle for Thanksgiving. The kids are fired up to beat these guys. I expect a very physical game."

Yet for the second consecutive year, Waterloo's start left observers speculating on whether the team had enjoyed too much turkey and stuffing at dinner. Vulcan forward Jay Moore scored 26 seconds into the game. The future University of Denver captain struck again at 8:41 during a power play. It was 4-1 at intermission, with a goal from Chris Scheid representing all of the Hawks' offense.

"We weren't ready to play," conceded Arf after the game. "They beat us to every loose puck, and we did not play our style of game. They wanted it more than we did."

Between 1980 and 2000, Jeff Arf was one of only two Black Hawks head coaches to stay with the club for three full seasons.

The Hawks did rally but missed two key chances to change the night's trajectory. Late in the first period, the Vulcans were whistled for two minors in less than a minute. Then early in the second, another pair of visitor penalties overlapped completely. Waterloo was unable to make productive use of either five-on-three situation. Brian Cook eventually brought the Hawks within two goals at 17:14, but it became a three-goal deficit again as St. Paul scored in the last minute before the second intermission.

The teams exchanged scores again during the first half of the third, but Moore completed his hat trick with 3:30 remaining, extending the lead to four for the first time and ending any further comeback hopes. With 21 St. Paul chances in the third period, goaltender Brett Klosowski faced 53 shots for the second consecutive Thanksgiving. Waterloo managed just 33 during an 0-for-9 night on the power play.

St. Paul   4 1 2 – 7
Waterloo   1 1 1 - 3

First Period – 1, St. Paul, Jay Moore (Rob Potter, Mike Harvey), :26. 2, St.

Paul, Moore (Sean Foley, Kevin Starren), 8:41 (pp). 3, St. Paul, Jim Pnewski (Mark Johnson, Jeff Miller), 9:09. 4, Waterloo, Chris Scheid (unassisted), 13:28. 5, St. Paul, Foley (Bill Coleman), 19:39. Penalties – R.J. Olson, StP (interference), 3:02; Harvey, StP (roughing), 7:41; Mike Notermann, Wat (roughing), 7:41; Kirk Haman, Wat (roughing) 7:55; Rob Brown, Wat (cross checking), 12:06; Mike Finnerty, StP (high sticking), 12:06; Olson, StP (holding), 16:32; Harvey, StP (cross checking), 17:24.

Second Period – 6, Waterloo, Brian Cook (Brown, Dick Reed), 17:14. 7, St. Paul, Pnewski (Finnerty, Rick Geehan), 19:23. Penalties – Dave Griffith, StP (interference), 3:10; bench minor, StP (delay of game), 3:10; Potter, StP (interference), 5:45; Scott Johnson, Wat (hooking), 6:10; Rob Kenny, Wat (holding), 10:16; Dan Michelsen, Wat (high sticking), 15:41; Potter, StP (holding), 15:41; S. Johnson, Wat (tripping), 17:22.

Third Period – 8, Waterloo, Bill Rooney (Mike Wickman), 4:21. 9, St. Paul, Foley (John Theraldson, Rick Aim), 8:02. 10, St. Paul, Moore (Potter, Theraldson), 16:30. Penalties – Harvey, StP (holding), 5:22; Reed, Wat (elbowing), 10:05; Moore, StP (delay of game), 13:25; Chris Hoffman, Wat (delay of game), 13:25; Michelsen, Wat (cross checking), 16:54; Lou Schaefer, StP (roughing), 18:31; Notermann, Wat (roughing), 18:31; Griffith, StP (holding), 18:41.

Shots on goal – St. Paul 17-15-21 53. Waterloo 11-10-12 33.

Goalies – St. Paul, Paul Osen (33-30); Waterloo, Brett Klosowski (53-46). Attendance – 941.

1987
Des Moines Buccaneers 8, Black Hawks 6

A few days before the Des Moines Buccaneers visited the Black Hawks to renew the teams' Thanksgiving acquaintance, Missouri Congressman Dick Gephardt was in both cities making campaign speeches. That Monday, Gephardt addressed a communication union in Des Moines, then visited Waterloo's UAW members to talk about worker rights and America's place in a globalizing, worldwide economy. Just over two months remained before the 1988 Iowa Caucuses.

For the first time since Iowa had come to full prominence in the presidential nominating process, Republicans and Democrats simultaneously needed to choose a candidate for an open seat in the Oval Office. The field was crowded with politicians on both sides of the political spectrum. Gephardt would win in Iowa, but the eventual Democratic nominee was Michael Dukakis (who finished third in the state). Bob Dole was the favorite among Iowa Republicans in February, however George H.W. Bush (like Dukakis, Iowa's third choice) earned the top spot on the ticket. The sitting vice president ultimately won the general election in November 1988.

The 1987 Thanksgiving game at McElroy Auditorium was equally unpredictable, and like the presidential race, early indications did not foretell the final outcome. The Black Hawks entered the matchup on a 4-0-1 run over the five preceding games. Waterloo started with a goal from Pat Rafferty at the 11-second mark. It was a welcome change after the Hawks had allowed a goal in the first minute of the two prior Thanksgiving contests.

Unfortunately, Des Moines swung in front with two goals separated by 90 seconds later in the period. Although the Hawks tied the score briefly, the Bucs were doubling-up Waterloo, 4-2, by intermission. Most of the second period was played with that score until Page Klostreich and Jon Rose eliminated the deficit in quick succession at 13:01 and 14:20 respectively. It was Rose's third point of the night, coming on top of two assists. Undaunted, Des Moines was back in the lead with a power play goal before the period ended and ahead by two again early in the third.

The Hawks drew closer at two different points in the final frame. More than 12 minutes remained when R.J. Olson scored to make it a 6-5 game. A disputed response from the Buccaneers pushed the visitors' lead to 7-5 at 16:06.

"That seventh goal should have never happened," Coach Jeff Arf said. "[Goaltender Todd Dietrich] had it smothered under his glove, but the whistle was slow, and they kept poking and poking until it came out."

Scott Krueger had the last whack which worked the puck across the goal line. It was his second of the game. The Hawks had just under four minutes to work with, and responded when Jay Boxer's long, unlikely chance eluded Bucs netminder Scott DeBaugh, nudging the margin back to one with 2:41 to go. Yet Krueger became the second opposing player in as many years to leave the building with a Thanksgiving hat trick, sealing the win with a distant attempt that still managed to find its way home despite a redirection.

The loss, plus another to the Sioux City Musketeers later in the weekend, were the Hawks' only two defeats in a ten-game span. Waterloo ended the year 20-25-3 after being 23-25-0 in 1986/87. The Hawks would not win 20 games in back-to-back seasons again until the new century.

Remnants of the 1988 Iowa Caucuses from the winning campaigns of Dick Gephardt and Bob Dole (pictured with his wife, Elizabeth). Dole button courtesy of the Robert and Elizabeth Dole Archive and Special Collections, Robert J. Dole Institute of Politics, University of Kansas.

Des Moines 4 1 3 – 8
Waterloo   2 2 2 – 6

First Period – 1, Waterloo, Pat Rafferty (Jon Rose), :11. 2, Des Moines, Mike Real (Bobby Nardella, Al Bouschor), 5:16; 3, Des Moines, Paul Hartke (Les Lundberg), 6:46. 4, Waterloo, Rob Kenny (Marc Gillard, Rose), 8:12. 5, Des Moines, Dave Norqual (Scott Krueger), 12:35. 6, Des Moines, Krueger (Don Reitz, Stu Vitue), 13:07. Penalties – none.

Second Period – 7, Waterloo, Page Klostreich (Paul Schwab, Kevin Manninen), 13:01. 8, Waterloo, Rose (Chris Hoffman, Kenny), 14:20. 9, Des Moines, Bouschor (Real, Krueger), 16:03 (pp). Penalties – Ray Kopitsch, DM (unsportsmanlike conduct), 2:16; Dan Michelsen, Wat (hooking), 3:13; Chris Hansen, DM (slashing), 9:24; Lloyd Houle, Wat (charging), 15:29; Scott DeBaugh, DM (delay of game), 18:21.

Third Period – 10, Des Moines, Nardella (Real, Kopitsch), 2:07. 11, Waterloo, R.J. Olson (Klostreich, Manninen), 7:42. 12, Des Moines, Krueger (Real), 16:06. 13, Waterloo, Jay Boxer (Gillard), 17:19. 14, Des Moines, Krueger (unassisted), 18:58 (en). Penalties – Reitz, DM (roughing), 6:44; Brian Wehr, Wat (holding), 6:44; Kopitsch, DM (tripping), 8:39.

Shots on goal – Des Moines 14-13-17 44. Waterloo 13-11-11 35.

Goalies – Des Moines, DeBaugh (35-29); Waterloo, Todd Dietrich (43-36).

Attendance – 842.

1988
Des Moines Buccaneers 8, Black Hawks 3

The Nintendo Entertainment System was on hundreds of Cedar Valley Christmas lists in 1988. On sale, the console retailed for $80 (games sold separately) and was priced competitively against rivals from Atari and Sega. Video cassette recorders, dot matrix printers, and handheld portable TVs were also sought-after tech gifts that season. Only the most affluent might have considered giving a cellular phone as service slowly expanded in Iowa: the mobile devices of the era – limited to functions similar to their corded home counterparts – retailed for over $800.

While technology was expensive relative to its performance, the shopping list for a Thanksgiving meal looks thrifty by modern standards. A feast of turkey (69¢ per pound), mashed potatoes ($1.99 for a ten pound bag), stuffing ($1.09 a box), cranberry sauce (49¢ a can), sweet potatoes (33¢ per pound), green beans (89¢ per pound), and pumpkin pie ($3.99 ready-to-eat) could have easily been prepared for a small family for under $30. Anyone on their own for the holiday could buy a single-serving version of a similar meal for $2.99, as long as they could make it to Hy-Vee by 2 o'clock.

Puck drop at McElroy Auditorium was at 7 p.m.

The Buccaneers (6-8-0) and Black Hawks (4-10-0) were both in the bottom half of the USHL standings and each among the league's lowest-scoring teams. Des Moines had defeated Sioux City at home the night before, while Waterloo had not played since the previous weekend. Nonetheless, the visitors had a better start, going ahead less than four minutes into the game. A follow-up goal in the last three minutes before intermission made it 2-0 during a period in which the Bucs outshot their hosts, 13-7.

Mick Kempffer's power play goal for the Hawks nearly three minutes into the second period brought Waterloo as close as they would be for the rest of the evening. The 2-1 score lasted until 6:36 before Des Moines began to blow the game open. The Bucs scored four times in less than nine minutes and fired 19 shots at Hawks goalie Chris Gordon, all either at even strength or while shorthanded.

Waterloo's Brian Wehr lunges toward the puck ahead of a pursuing opponent.

Greg Brown / Waterloo-Cedar Falls Courier.

"When the whole team is standing around and nobody is hitting, it's hard to pinpoint one or two things that you're doing wrong," said new Head Coach Nick Whelihan (who had played against Waterloo for the Green Bay Bobcats in the 1980 Thanksgiving matchup), "But the last two games, we haven't demonstrated any intensity whatsoever."

The third period was a draw. Waterloo's Chris Brown converted a power play chance at 4:15, but on the following shift, Stu Vitue notched a goal, to go with two earlier assists. The final goals of the game were also scored in quick succession in the closing minutes. Tony Stoskopf briefly extended the margin to six goals, but former Waterloo Columbus forward Brian Wehr provided a final highlight after an interval of just 62 seconds. Despite having six power plays (resulting in two goals), the Black Hawks were still outshot 50-29. The Buccaneers would win four of five games against the Hawks in 1988/89; they recorded video game-like numbers, scoring at least eight goals in each victory.

Des Moines   2 4 2 – 8
Waterloo   0 1 2 – 3

First Period – 1, Des Moines, Mike Real (Sean Wilmert), 3:41. 2, Des Moines, Pete Helgeson (Al Bouschor, Wilmert), 17:02. Penalties – Stu Vitue, DM (unsportsmanlike conduct), 3:26; Brian Wehr, Wat (roughing), 3:26; Dennis Ryan, Wat (holding), 11:06.

Second Period – 3, Waterloo, Mick Kempffer (Mark Erkkila, Cory Metro), 2:51 (pp). 4, Des Moines, Mike Hauswirth (Jim Brignall, Lloyd Houle), 6:36. 5, Des Moines, Robb Johnson (Vitue, Wilmert), 7:19. 6, Des Moines, Brignall (Hauswirth), 13:38. 7, Des Moines, Real (Vitue), 15:16. Penalties – Bouschor, DM (roughing), 2:01; Charlie Elliott, DM (cross checking), 9:11.

Third Period – 8, Waterloo, Chris Brown (Kevin Quinn, Todd Waldo), 4:15 (pp). 9, Des Moines, Vitue (Wilmert, Sean Murdoch), 4:27. 10, Des Moines, Tony Stoskopf (Murdoch), 16:41. 11, Waterloo, Wehr (Kevin Manninen, Rick Davis), 17:43. Penalties – Dave Norqual, DM (interference), 4:09; Russ Johnson, DM (elbowing), 4:52; Eric Olson, Wat (slashing), 8:21; Elliott, DM (slashing), 8:21; Elliott, DM (cross checking), 8:21; Houle, DM (holding), 13:42.

Shots on goal – Des Moines 13-19-18 50. Waterloo 7-11-11 29.

Goalies – Des Moines, Jeff Markham (29-26); Waterloo, Chris Gordon (50-42).

Attendance – n/a.

1989
Black Hawks 5, North Iowa Huskies 4

Like the Black Hawks, the North Iowa Huskies were owned and operated by their local youth hockey association. Founded in 1983, the Huskies were the featured winter tenant in Mason City's North Iowa Recreational Arena, located (also similarly to Waterloo) within the local fairgrounds. Bob Motzko represented another tie between the Hawks and their closest geographic rival: the former Waterloo forward had been hired as an assistant by the Huskies prior to the start of their inaugural season, and returned as head coach during the winter of 1986/87. Motzko brought North Iowa a level of success Waterloo could never achieve during the era when USHL teams participated in USA Hockey's National Junior Tournament. In the spring of 1989, the Huskies won that event. That autumn, they visited McElroy Auditorium as the defending national champions in the first of four Thanksgiving appearances through the end of the 1990s.

By comparison, the Hawks had missed the 1988/89 playoffs, and the new season was offering little opportunity for optimism. By late November, Waterloo was 2-14-1, including a pair of losses against North Iowa. The Hawks had fallen in five straight games prior to hosting the Huskies for what would prove to be the last of 18 consecutive Thanksgiving contests on the Cattle Congress grounds.

Despite the team's poor record a year earlier, goaltender Chris Gordon had still been named an All-Star and recognized on the All-USHL Second Team at the end of the season. In Gordon's second Thanksgiving appearance, the Huskies put one past him 4:32 into the first period, but the 6-foot Sault Ste. Marie, Michigan, native was strong the rest of the way, and the Hawks gave him a lead to work with before intermission. Waterloo's short but significant offensive flurry came during a 22-second window near the middle of the period. A follow-up shot by Brad Johnson tied the game; then on the next shift, a pair of defensemen connected for a goal when John Gruden's pass allowed Chris Oleson to hurry the puck up the ice for a go-ahead score.

"We didn't have any first period blues," noted Coach Nick Whelihan as the Hawks outshot the Huskies 13-10. "We've had a lot of games where we've just buried ourselves early and then come back to fall one goal short."

Instead, a second productive period allowed Waterloo to stay out of reach. Gruden's second assist helped the Hawks make it 3-1 less than five minutes after the break when Mike Leier scored on a rebound. Although the Huskies answered two-and-a-half minutes later, Waterloo native Brian Wehr hit the net to give the Hawks a two-goal lead once more at 13:06. It took 16 Gordon saves to sustain that margin.

The Hawks sprang out of the second intermission to stretch the lead to three in the first minute of the third. Todd Turcotte provided a vital goal which proved to be the winner. All three of the Huskies' power plays followed during the final 20 minutes, and North Iowa scored on two of them, including a goal with a sixth attacker and 31 seconds to go. However, Gordon produced 21 more saves for a total of 46 in the victory. It was the second consecutive Thanksgiving game in which he faced 50 opposing shots and his final win for Waterloo before joining the Omaha Lancers later that season.

Chris Gordon was one of several Black Hawks goalies who played better than the statistics might suggest as Waterloo struggled through much of the 1980s.

Photo courtesy of Michigan Athletics.

North Iowa   1 1 2 – 4
Waterloo   2 2 1 – 5

First Period – 1, North Iowa, Cory Lindvall (Steve Nelson, Jason Mack),

4:32. 2, Waterloo, Brad Johnson (Craig Hollenbeck), 11:05. 3, Waterloo, Chris Oleson (John Gruden), 11:27. Penalties – none.

Second Period – 4, Waterloo, Mike Leier (Jason Navarro, Gruden), 4:45. 5, North Iowa, Tom Friberg (Kevin Dillard), 7:13. 6, Waterloo, Brian Wehr (Todd Turcotte, Steve Nelson), 13:06. Penalties – none.

Third Period – 7, Waterloo, Turcotte (Brad Beedle), :47. 8, North Iowa, Corey Grassel (Dave Nystrom, Chris Morque), 5:20 (pp). 9, North Iowa, Nelson (Brian Lyke), 19:29 (pp). Penalties – Shawn Wienke, Wat (hooking), 3:51; Wienke, Wat (cross checking), 13:14; Morque, NI (misconduct), 16:42; Wienke, Wat (charging), 18:54.

Shots on goal – North Iowa 10-17-23 50. Waterloo 13-8-8 29.

Goalies – North Iowa, Mike Beaton (29-24); Waterloo, Chris Gordon (50-46).

Attendance – n/a.

1992
Black Hawks 2, Sioux City Musketeers 2 (OT)

In the hiatus between Thanksgiving games, the City of Waterloo and the National Cattle Congress board discussed several alternatives for a new rink to replace McElroy Auditorium. The ice infrastructure in the old building was 30 years old and disintegrating. In a worst-case scenario, city officials suggested the foundation under McElroy might degrade to a state where the Auditorium could fall down. However, the NCC was already under a financial strain as it tried to keep Waterloo Greyhound Park open and would have been unable to contribute much to a new rink project. By the summer of 1992, it was evident that Waterloo hockey would not be played in a Cattle Congress facility much longer.

City officials weighed at least 17 different locations for a new arena in all corners of the community. Both ends of Highway 63 were considered – near Allen Hospital to the north and the racetrack to the south – as well as multiple sites near the Cedar River, close to the airport, Central Middle School, or the former Rath Packing Company. By the beginning of hockey season, the most likely property was a block at the intersection of Jefferson and 6th Streets. That portion of Waterloo was already scheduled for substantial changes with the construction of a new six-lane Highway 218 thruway.

The plan would have dislodged several businesses between Sixth and Seventh Street, and the owners vocally objected. Other Cedar Valley sports fans were unhappy that the city was willing to back a new arena while the Waterloo Diamonds' home at Municipal (now Riverfront) Stadium fell short of minor league baseball standards, making it likely that the Midwest League would soon relocate the club. Another collection of residents thought the community should focus its money and attention on more essential services. Many ice arena-backers doubted a referendum on the project could pass at the required 60 percent level and hoped to avoid putting the issue up for a vote. By Thanksgiving, momentum was in danger of stalling.

Meanwhile, the Black Hawks – under new ownership and led by first-year coach Scott Mikesch – seemed to be coming around on the ice. McElroy's poor condition had forced the team to hold its preseason practices in Ames, Des Moines, and Mason City. Waterloo went winless during their first five games but had improved to 5-8-2 by the time the Sioux City Musketeers came across the state on November 26th.

After considerable discussion about the site of the rink, Young Arena was eventually planned and constructed on Commercial Street. Artist rendering provided by INVISION Architecture.

A solid effort by Adam Brouk early in the first, and a pinpoint pass from Jason Blake to Todd Steinmetz at nearly the same time in the second, gave Waterloo a 2-0 lead. The Musketeers rallied on special teams, then tied the game early in the third. The matchup might have swung to the visitors several times during the final frame and overtime as Sioux City outshot the Hawks 28-8 after the second intermission. However Paul Spencer's sensational effort allowed Waterloo to earn a point.

"[Sioux City goalie Brian] Leitza and Spencer both had outstanding performances," Mikesch said approvingly after the game, "We didn't tie because both teams didn't have their chances, the goalies just had big nights."

While the November stalemate between the Hawks and Musketeers could not be settled beyond a draw, the arena question was resolved in February. The Young family – owners of several businesses in Waterloo – donated property between 1st Street and Mullen Avenue, plus millions of dollars in construction expenses, for the new rink. The completed building would eventually be named in their honor, and the ground was broken for the facility later in 1993.

Sioux City   0 1 1 0 – 2
Waterloo   1 1 0 0 – 2

First Period – 1, Waterloo, Adam Brouk (Duane Roe), 4:02. Penalties – Ben Stadey, Wat (cross checking), 7:31.

Second Period – 2, Waterloo, Todd Steinmetz (Jason Blake), 3:37. 3, Sioux City, David Buck (Derek Locker, Marc Grande), 6:33 (pp). Penalties – Aaron Broten, Wat (roughing), 6:09; Brian Folden, Wat (checking from behind), 7:59. Chris Chelios, SC (holding), 10:48; Blake, Wat (holding) 19:15; Jason Dekker, Wat (roughing), 20:00; Erik Raygor, SC (roughing), 20:00.

Third Period – 4, Sioux City, Mike Rotch (unassisted), 1:50. Penalties – Bryon Haro, SC (hooking), 4:41; Blake, Wat (interference), 5:57; Blake, Wat (fighting), 13:02; Blake, Wat (game misconduct), 13:02; Jesse Monell, SC (fighting), 13:02; Monell, SC (game misconduct), 13:02; Scott Bachinski, Wat (holding), 17:56; Grande, SC (holding), 17:56.

Overtime – no scoring. Penalties – none.

Shots on goal – Sioux City 9-14-17-11 51. Waterloo 13-9-6-4 32.

Goalies – Sioux City, Brian Leitza (32-30); Waterloo, Paul Spencer (51-49).

Attendance – 1,269.

1993
Black Hawks 3, North Iowa Huskies 2 (OT)

Brian Folden joined the Black Hawks at nearly the final moment before the 1992/93 season. Typically used as a checking, stay-at-home defenseman, the 6-foot-2-inch, 220-pound Fargo native was also versatile enough to skate on right wing. Despite his late arrival and modest offense, Folden was chosen to play in the 1992/93 USHL All-Star Game. The Hawks finished seventh that year, qualifying for the postseason. A significant number of players – including Folden, forwards Jason Blake, Todd Steinmetz, Bobby Hayes, Chris Coakley, and several others – returned to Waterloo in the fall of 1993.

During their second USHL season together, this group of Black Hawks anchored the most formidable Waterloo team since the league's first year with all-junior rosters. They won six of their first eight games. A victory while visiting the North Iowa Huskies on the night before Thanksgiving bumped their record to 11-5-0. It was a win total which already equaled or surpassed that which the club had achieved in five of the 13 seasons after Jack Barzee had left Waterloo. The Wednesday night 7-6 overtime result in Mason City had included Folden's first USHL goal and gave the Hawks their second five-game winning streak of the young campaign.

The rematch in Waterloo the next night began with a scoreless, penalty-free first period. The last place Huskies nudged in front at 9:12 of the second period and owned a 2-1 lead after 40 minutes. What's more, North Iowa was outshooting the Hawks 23-22 at that point. Their lead held through much of the third period.

In the standings, the Hawks were trying to close in on the USHL-leading Des Moines Buccaneers and also extend their string of victories to match the club's best junior-era run. Besides that, another notable accomplishment hung in the balance as the third period whizzed by. Coakley was in danger of a 15-

game point streak unceremoniously ending. There had been no drama about his personal accomplishments the night before in Mason City. In that game, he had assisted on Folden's goal in the first minute of play.

Coakley's crucial Thanksgiving point finally came with under four minutes to go. North Iowa goalie Scott McKee could not soak up Blake's initial shot. Coakley pounced for the game-tying goal after the Hawks had been building pressure for several minutes.

"That's what we'd been missing for most of the game," said Coach Scott Mikesch. "We weren't finishing checks or getting a good second effort on our shots. Sometimes it's better to be lucky than good, and we've been very lucky these last two nights."

With nearly 1,800 fans coming to life behind them, Waterloo generated more chances late in regulation and into the early part of the 10-minute overtime. McKee pushed his save count to 38 before the Hawks created an odd-man chance he couldn't stop.

With 2:22 left before the game would have ended in a tie, Blake attracted two defenders in the neutral zone. The future NHL All-Star threaded a pass to Jeff Kozakowski as the Hawks suddenly found themselves with a three-on-one look. Kozakowski slipped the puck to Folden, and for the second straight night, the big North Dakotan produced a goal.

Brian Folden's timely goal against North Iowa sealed Waterloo's first overtime win during a Thanksgiving game after two ties (1972 and 1992) and a loss (1983).

Folden scored five more times that season. Blake, Kozakowski, and goalie Terry Jarkowsky were each chosen for All-USHL honors. The Black Hawks finished with 33 wins, their third-highest total in any year up to that time, including the seasons featuring senior players. Meanwhile, North Iowa struggled through 1993/94, but better things – and many more Thanksgiving games – awaited third-year Huskies Head Coach P.K. O'Handley.

North Iowa   0 2 0 0 – 2
Waterloo   0 1 1 1 – 3

First Period – no scoring. Penalties – none.

Second Period – 1, North Iowa, Jeremy Asheim (Troy Torrence), 9:12. 2, Waterloo, Marty Laurila (Rod Butler, Jon Garver), 14:30. 3, North Iowa, Chris Hvinden (Asheim, Tim Walsh), 19:48. Penalties – Bobby Hayes, Wat (interference), 4:14.

Third Period – 4, Waterloo, Chris Coakley (Jason Blake, Brent Bessey), 16:11. Penalties – none.

Overtime – 5, Waterloo, Brian Folden (Blake, Jeff Kozakowski), 7:38. Penalties – none.

Shots on goal – North Iowa 9-14-7-2 32. Waterloo 10-12-12-7 41.

Goalies – North Iowa, Scott McKee (41-38); Waterloo, Terry Jarkowsky (32-30).

Attendance – 1,795.

1994
Wisconsin Capitols 6, Black Hawks 3

Many sports fans had more reasons for disappointment than thankfulness in November of 1994. A Major League Baseball strike had begun in August and meant that the World Series was not played for the first time in 90 years. Waterloo's ballpark had been quiet and dark all summer after the Waterloo Diamonds baseball club was relocated. The National Hockey League season, which should have been nearly two months old, had not started due to a labor dispute. That situation led Black Hawks General Manager Scott Brand to note glibly that Waterloo's attendance of 19,346 through eight home games was better than all of the NHL's clubs combined.

Whether it was the absence of other sports alternatives, or a response to the team's success in 1993/94, or a nostalgic yearning to see the final series of games in McElroy Auditorium, the Hawks' attendance was up. The Thanksgiving matchup with Wisconsin was one of three games left in the building before the team would relocate to Young Arena after Christmas. A Thanksgiving crowd of 2,819 was over a thousand more than the audience for the 1993 game.

Jason Blake was reportedly part of the group in the stands. The 1993/94 USHL Player of the Year was a freshman at Ferris State and returned for a holiday visit. The Hawks were missing Blake and many of his teammates from the previous year. Waterloo had started the new season 5-9-1, just ahead of the 5-12-0 Wisconsin Capitols.

Wisconsin went ahead briefly in the first period, before Hawks forward Roger Trudeau tied the matchup. Although the teams were even with a 1-1 score at intermission, the game swung decisively to the Capitols in the second. Former Dubuque Fighting Saint winger Eric Tuott had not recorded a goal since being acquired as the season was getting underway, but he had two for

Wisconsin in the period. Those scores were bookended by goals from top Wisconsin offensive threat Darren Clark and J.B. L'Esperance (who, like Tuott, also hadn't previously scored that season).

"It seems like whatever can go wrong is going wrong...we're not working hard enough to create breaks," lamented Hawks Coach Scott Mikesch, adding, "We're not a very mature team right now."

The Capitols recorded their fifth consecutive goal 33 seconds into the third period to open up a 6-1 lead. The frustrating night went on to include a series of fights, with five players sent to the dressing room before the game was over.

It was an unlikely evening to make a good first impression, but new forward Mark Giannetti managed to do it. The Hawks had acquired Giannetti from the Detroit Freeze of the North American Hockey League earlier in the week. The 5-foot-11-inch forward who had also previously played for the Sudbury Wolves in the Ontario Hockey League assisted on Trudeau's first period goal. Then at 14:27 of the third, he added one of his own for a two-point Waterloo debut. Veteran Todd Steinmetz notched a closing goal in the final minute with the outcome long since decided.

In his first Black Hawks appearance, Mark Giannetti recorded two points Here he duels with Madison's Cort Lundeen; both players scored during the third period.

Dan Nierling / Waterloo-Cedar Falls Courier.

The loss was part of an 11-game winless streak, which included defeats during Waterloo's final games at McElroy Auditorium in the weeks which followed.

Wisconsin   1 4 1 – 6
Waterloo   1 0 2 – 3

First Period – 1, Wisconsin, Tony Cinquegrano (Mike Skogland, Darren Clark), 5:37. 2, Waterloo, Roger Trudeau (Mark Giannetti, Jeff Kozakowski), 8:44.

Second Period – 3, Wisconsin, Clark (Cort Lundeen, Skogland), 4:32. 4, Wisconsin, Eric Tuott (Andrew Jurkowski), 10:40. 5, Wisconsin, Tuott (Luke Murray, Brant Buchholz), 13:18. 6, Wisconsin, J.B. L'Esperance (Cinquegrano, Jurkowski), 13:51.

Third Period – 7, Wisconsin, Lundeen (Clark, Skogland), :23. 8, Waterloo, Giannetti (Evan Sylvester, Billy Zuccaro), 14:27. 9, Waterloo, Todd Steinmetz (unassisted), 19:27.

Goalies – Wisconsin, Forrest Karr (29-27); Waterloo, Jeff Melnechuk & Scott Swanjord (33-27).

Attendance – 2,819.

(Note – penalties and shots-by-period are not available).

1997
Black Hawks 4, North Iowa Huskies 0

Since Waterloo did not host Thanksgiving hockey in 1995 or 1996, Young Arena's first game on the holiday was played nearly two full years after the new rink opened. The building on Commercial Street had the biggest ice surface in the USHL. Hawks players and fans were excited to enjoy the new amenities, and the team celebrated relatively solid home success, even while their overall record lagged in the mid-1990s. Entering 1997/98, Waterloo had missed the playoffs in two of the three previous years.

The 1997 game was a renewal of Waterloo's Thanksgiving rivalry with the North Iowa Huskies. Although North Iowa remained the nearest USHL destination to Waterloo, the Huskies had landed on the other side of the league's divisional divide. As a result, the teams were scheduled to meet just four times in 1997/98. Regardless, the first matchup a month earlier had been memorable: the Hawks scratched out a 3-2 win, and a postgame confrontation on the ice nearly turned into a brawl outside the locker room under the bleachers.

Goalie Phil Osaer had made 30 saves in the first meeting and was given the start again on Thanksgiving. The 17-year-old from the Detroit suburbs was among the youngest Black Hawks that winter. He hadn't begun playing goalie until age nine but quickly showed a flair for the position. The future USHL All-Star and St. Louis Blues draft pick would deliver one of his finest games as a Black Hawk in front of the sellout holiday crowd.

The Huskies buzzed 14 shots Osaer's direction during the first period, but he stopped them all. Meanwhile, Waterloo staked their netminder to a 2-0 lead. Veteran Ryan Hale scored early and B.J. Stephens – just added in a trade from the Rochester Mustangs earlier in November – notched a goal nearly eight minutes later. The weight of scoring chances flipped in the second period; Waterloo outshot the Huskies 13-3 and added an unassisted goal from Tom Ogee to make the score 3-0.

Osaer still had to be sharp in the third period to keep the Hawks on top. Waterloo's lead increased at 2:54 when Matt Chandler beat Gregg Naumenko on one of only three Black Hawks chances. At the other end of the ice, North Iowa generated 15 shots in the final 20 minutes – almost all of them at even strength – to keep the future Ferris State Bulldog occupied. Osaer's 32-save shutout was the first time Waterloo had whitewashed an opponent on Thanksgiving since 1966.

Osaer's shutout of North Iowa was one of two times he would blank an opponent in 1997/98. He also did it with 29 saves in an 8-0 Black Hawks win versus the Dubuque Fighting Saints in January.

Young Arena's first Thanksgiving game was quickly followed by another first for the facility. After holiday weekend skating activities concluded, dozens of workers slid the scoreboard from its normal position over center ice to the east end of the building, covered the playing surface with plywood, and laid out a basketball court. That Monday night, 1,800 noisy UNI Panther fans brought their purple and gold attire to the rink for the first NCAA men's basketball game in the building. Their reverberating cheers made the event much louder that what was possible with a bigger crowd in the airy environment of the UNI-Dome, and the Panthers rolled to an easy 79-61 win over the UMKC Kangaroos.

North Iowa   0 0 0 – 0
Waterloo   2 1 1 – 4
First Period – 1, Waterloo, Ryan Hale (Steve Savre, Matt Murray), 3:51. 2, Waterloo, B.J. Stephens (Matt Chandler), 11:33. Penalties – Keith Stanich,

Wat (tripping), 13:51; Shaun Winkler, NI (interference), 14:07.

Second Period – 3, Waterloo, Tom Ogee (unassisted), 13:52. Penalties – Dave Almquist, NI (checking from behind), 3:07; Almquist, NI (game misconduct), 3:07; Kyle O'Keefe, Wat (slashing), 4:55; Jeff Crouse, NI (cross checking), 4:55; Tom Nelson, NI (unsportsmanlike conduct), 8:48; Chris Von Trzcinski, Wat (unsportsmanlike conduct), 8:48.

Third Period – 4, Waterloo, Chandler (Von Trzcinski, Mike LaRocca), 2:54 (pp). Penalties – Saysona Phrakonkhma, NI (slashing), 1:25; Von Trzcinski, Wat (tripping), 5:05.

Shots on goal – North Iowa 14-3-15 32. Waterloo 8-13-3 24.

Goalies – North Iowa, Gregg Naumenko (23-19), Rob Anderson (1-1); Waterloo, Phil Osaer (32-32).

Attendance – 2,979.

1998
Black Hawks 4, North Iowa Huskies 1

Waterloo's afternoon high temperature on Thanksgiving in 1998 was a remarkably pleasant 67, blasting past the previous record for that date by five degrees. Neither the Black Hawks nor the North Iowa Huskies could claim to be that hot, with each team well below .500 when they arrived at the rink around sunset. However, the Hawks had made the most of a chance to warm up; 1998 was the first year Waterloo ever played at home on the Wednesday before a Thanksgiving contest instead of being on the road. The team had taken advantage by surprising the Sioux City Musketeers for a shootout win at Young Arena.

The 1997 and 1998 Thanksgiving games were the only time during the 1990s when the Hawks faced the same opponent in consecutive years. The 1998 game was also a playoff rematch. That spring, North Iowa had eliminated Waterloo in five games during a best-of-seven series. The Hawks and Huskies (coincidentally, each owned by Butch Johnson) had both experienced substantial changes since then. North Iowa's were arguably more significant, and included the departure of Head Coach P.K. O'Handley for professional hockey after seven seasons in Mason City.

The Huskies had a ragged start. They were credited with only two shots in the scoreless opening period, despite an early power play. The previous night, Hawks goalie Nate Nomeland had been called on to make more saves than that during the shootout portion of Waterloo's win against Sioux City.

Luke Fulghum notched the Hawks' opening goal, creating his scoring chance from behind the North Iowa net two minutes into the second period. Cale Finseth followed by pushing in a loose rebound to make it 2-0 at 6:37. While Waterloo had the tangible results, it was also a much livelier period for the Huskies, who swatted 16 shots Nomeland's way, but to no avail.

Luke Fulghum and the Black Hawks were excited to jump in front of North Iowa early in the second period. The back-to-back wins versus the Huskies were Waterloo's first on consecutive Thanksgivings in more than a decade.

Jack Jorgensen / Waterloo-Cedar Falls Courier.

The home team continued to click offensively in the third. John Grubb had set up Fulghum's initial score, and Grubb added one of his own with 15:40 remaining. Brian Canady's power play goal at 11:18 put the score where it had been when the teams met on the same holiday 364 days earlier.

Unfortunately, Nomeland's bid to match Phil Osaer's 1997 result fell 50 seconds short. Tom Stone shattered the shutout during a five-on-three power play in the final minute. Nomeland finished with the win and 28 saves.

"Good teams put three good periods together, and we didn't quite get that done," observed Scott Pionk after his second Thanksgiving win as the Hawks' head coach. "I did like the way we responded in the third period. We used more players than they did. We might have worn them down a little bit."

The midweek victories opened a six-game Hawks homestand, but Waterloo lost the next four and earned only one more win before the year flipped to 1999. They would not hold an opponent to one goal again until February. The Huskies hardly fared better, finishing with 18 wins as both clubs missed the playoffs. The Thanksgiving game was the last time North Iowa visited Young Arena before relocating to Cedar Rapids the next summer.

North Iowa   0 0 1 – 1
Waterloo   0 2 2 – 4

First Period – no scoring. Penalties – bench minor, Wat (too many men), 2:17; Nick Anderson, NI (hooking), 10:22.

Second Period – 1, Waterloo, Luke Fulghum (John Grubb, Brian Knaeble), 2:00. 2, Waterloo, Cale Finseth (Ryan Hale, Mike Bujdos), 6:37. Penalties – Finseth, Wat (elbowing), 9:16.

Third Period – 3, Waterloo, Grubb (Knaeble), 4:20. 4, Waterloo, Brian Canady (Keith Stanich, Bujdos), 11:18 (pp). 5, North Iowa, Tom Stone (Garrett Rogstad, Anderson), 19:10 (pp). Penalties – Mike Noel, NI (roughing), 2:04; Anderson, NI (cross checking), 10:19; Tom Ogee, Wat (holding), 17:11; Jake Tesar, Wat (roughing), 18:42.

Shots on goal – North Iowa 2-16-11 29. Waterloo 9-9-25 43.

Goalies – North Iowa, Willie Raderschadt (43-39); Waterloo, Nate Nomeland (29-28).

Attendance – 2,307.

1999
Rochester Mustangs 6, Black Hawks 2

Downtown retail areas dueled with shopping malls for Cedar Valley holiday customers throughout the 1970s and into the 80s. At that point, large national retailers like Wal-Mart began to challenge them both. By 1999, every store with a physical location expected competition from the internet. During that Christmas shopping season, quarterly online sales were expected to (and ultimately did) surpass $5 billion dollars for the first time. Amazon was quickly becoming a well-known brand, although many other e-commerce hopefuls would soon disappear in the stock market crash associated with the "dot-com bubble."

The start of hockey season in 1999 represented a bubble of sorts for the Black Hawks. Waterloo lost in regulation only once during the first five weeks of the schedule and earned 18 of 22 possible points from the first 11 games. New coach Scott Koberinski, goaltending acquisition Darren Gastrock, and veteran forward Luke Fulghum were among the notable figures involved in the turnaround.

"Xs and Os don't mean a whole lot to me. It's a simple game. I try not to complicate things," Koberinski said after he was hired to replace Scott Pionk days before the start of the season. "I would call myself a players' coach. I get along with the kids and I want them to feel like they can come and talk to me. We're going to work our tails off, but we're also going to have some fun."

Despite taking a few more losses in November, the team was likely still having fun by Thanksgiving. Their 11-5-2 record put them second in the USHL East Division, behind only the U.S. National Team Development Program Under-18s.

Like a 6-0 loss to the NTDP on Halloween, Waterloo's Thanksgiving defeat by Rochester would be one of only a few significant early setbacks. The game swung on a Mustang surge in the late second and early third periods. Before that, goals by Rochester's Pascal Appel and Waterloo's Brian Knaeble canceled each other when they were scored just over a minute apart in the first period.

The next 20 minutes were entirely one-sided.

Rochester outshot the Hawks 12-1 in the middle period. The Mustangs went ahead permanently at 5:35, controlling an offensive zone draw that resulted in a Tom Erickson goal. After keeping the Hawks within one for much of the second, Gastrock was lifted after allowing both a breakaway goal by Aaron Gill with 2:25 left in the period and then a Kyle Cash follow-up 45 seconds later. Rheese Carlson's power play goal 1:05 into the third was one of two times he would strike for Rochester in the final period. The Hawks' John Grubb wedged-in Waterloo's only response between Carlson's goals.

"After starting off great this year, we haven't had that for a while," said Koberinski when his team had left the ice. "I think we've got some people who think they're better than they really are. When you start thinking like that, you're in trouble."

Thanksgiving was not kind to Scott Koberinski, who currently holds the unfortunate distinction of being the only Waterloo coach to lose on the holiday in three straight years.

The Hawks were able to remain near the top of the East Division through the holidays and past the first month of 2000. However, after Valentine's Day, their results crumbled. The regular season, which had begun so well, ended with Waterloo winning just three times in the last 13 games. In the playoffs, the seventh-seeded Hawks won the first matchup during a series against the Green Bay Gamblers, but were ushered out of the postseason with three losses in the days which followed.

Rochester   1 3 2 – 6
Waterloo   1 0 1 – 2

First Period – 1, Rochester, Pascal Appel (Kyle Cash), 13:34. 2, Waterloo, Brian Knaeble (Michal Hudec), 14:41 (pp). Penalties – Brian Canady, Wat (roughing), :14; Rheese Carlson, Roc (slashing), 6:23; Canady, Wat (delay of game), 7:18; Jeremy Downs, Roc (delay of game), 7:18; Jim Murphy, Wat (high sticking), 7:24; Jesse Modahl, Roc (elbowing), 14:36; Murphy, Wat (roughing), 20:00; Dax Leepart, Roc (roughing), 20:00.

Second Period – 3, Rochester, Tom Erickson (Nate Markus, Aaron Gill), 5:36. 4, Rochester, Gill (unassisted), 17:35. 5, Rochester, Cash (Leepart), 18:20 (pp). Penalties – Adam Rhein, Wat (cross checking), 6:11; bench minor, Wat (too many men), 14:04; Joe Zuccaro, Wat (boarding major), 18:53; Zuccaro, Wat (ejection), 18:53.

Third Period – 6, Rochester, Carlson (Gill), 1:05 (pp). 7, Waterloo, John Grubb (Tom Galvin), 10:14 (pp). 8, Rochester, Carlson (David Nelson), 13:44. Penalties – Carlson, Roc (hooking), 3:32; Cash, Roc (interference), 9:53; Hudec, Wat (hooking), 11:40; Joel Starke, Roc (roughing), 14:05; Grubb, Wat (roughing), 14:05; Erickson, Roc (high sticking), 16:19; Erickson, Roc (fighting), 16:19; Erickson, Roc (game misconduct), 16:19; Canady, Wat (fighting), 16:19; Canady, Wat (game misconduct), 16:19; Downs, Roc (holding), 17:57; Hudec, Wat (holding), 17:57.

Shots on goal – Rochester 10-12-10 32. Waterloo 7-1-8 16.

Goalies – Rochester, Adam Coole (16-14); Waterloo, Darren Gastrock (22-18), Adam Hanna (10-8).

Attendance – 2,396.

2000
Cedar Rapids RoughRiders 4, Black Hawks 3

The typical United States Hockey League season is about two months old by the time Thanksgiving arrives. In the all-junior USHL, the holiday can produce a moment of homesickness. For rookies especially, time away from family may be particularly hard on a day dedicated to gathering together with relatives and loved-ones.

International players might not have any sentimental attachment to the fourth Thursday in November, but wistfulness for the familiar surroundings of home is a feeling they typically understand. Beginning in the late 1990s, the USHL saw a steadily increasing number of exceptional European players. Ruslan Fedotenko (Sioux City), Rostislav Klesla (Sioux City), and Thomas Vanek (Sioux Falls) each spent productive seasons in the league on their way to notable NHL careers. The stories of these international prodigies coming to Midwestern towns was intriguing enough to entice the USHL to change its All-Star format to "USA versus the World" for several seasons (although a limited number of international roster spots prevented the league from staying completely true to those designations). One of the best European players in Waterloo in those days was defenseman Lubos Velebny.

At age 18 when he joined the Hawks, Velebny was from Slovakia. He had been chosen in the seventh round of the 2000 NHL Draft by the Toronto Maple Leafs, and at 6-feet-2-inches and 190 pounds, Velebny projected the stature of a pro player. His English was limited, and difficulties processing the documents to complete his transfer across the Atlantic proved to be a challenge which cost him some time in the lineup. Nevertheless, Velebny was named USHL Defenseman of the Week by the close of October and joined future NHL'er Andrew Alberts to give the Hawks a formidable blueline tandem.

Two-and-a-half minutes into Waterloo's first Thanksgiving game against the Cedar Rapids RoughRiders, Velebny set up the opening goal by Ryan Markham. The visitors tied the score with just over eight minutes to play, but Velebny collected his second point of the night on Brian Canady's power play goal at 15:41. His name was read over the PA system a third time when he slipped a pass to Trevor Wolfe and notched another special teams assist in the mid-second period.

RoughRider goaltender Bobby Goepfert didn't allow the Black Hawk to score again, with or without help from Velebny.

Through two periods, Waterloo owned a 3-2 lead, and the Hawks were outshooting Cedar Rapids 30-19. The penalty-filled game (31 minors were called) turned on the night's third "too many men on the ice" call (Canady's first period goal had given Waterloo the lead when Cedar Rapids was whistled for the same infraction). With the Hawks shorthanded after making a bad change, Danny O'Brien tied it at 12:19 of the third. Then Gerry Hickey's blast five-and-a-half minutes later proved to be the game-winner, as Goepfert stopped all of Waterloo's late chances for a 37-save comeback victory.

Just over a month later, Velebny would represent Slovakia during the first of two appearances at the World Junior Championships. Despite being out of the Hawks' lineup for that competition and missing a total of 11 games throughout the season, Velebny still accumulated 36 points (11 goals, 25 assists) in 45 appearances to rank fourth on the Waterloo roster and tie for fourth in scoring among all USHL defensemen. After a season in the Cedar Valley, he spent the following year in the Ontario Hockey League. The vast majority of Velebny's long professional career has been played in Europe.

By the time this pocket schedule was printed, the Black Hawks had settled into Young Arena, with the building's nickname and goal song well-established.

From the collection of Bob Batcheller; see more at thebatchellerpad.com.

Cedar Rapids   1 1 2 – 4
Waterloo   2 1 0 – 3

First Period – 1, Waterloo, Ryan Markham (Lubos Velebny, John Grubb), 2:26. 2, Cedar Rapids, Jeremy Wilson (Xavier Daramy), 11:47. 3, Waterloo, Brian Canady (Trevor Wolfe, Velebny), 15:41 (pp). Penalties – Gerry Hickey, CR (roughing), 4:15; Chris Snavely, CR (delay of game), 6:59, Craig Falite, Wat (delay of game), 6:59; Kyle Cash, Wat (hooking), 8:50; Derrick Johnson, CR (holding), 14:41; bench minor, CR (too many men), 15:12; Luke Fulghum, Wat (interference), 15:58; P.J. Atherton, CR (roughing), 16:21.

Second Period – 4, Waterloo, Wolfe (Velebny, Markham), 7:37 (pp). 5, Cedar Rapids, Ted O'Leary (Atherton, Marc Andre Lalande), 7:53. Penalties – Mike Patton, CR (roughing), 4:12; Greg Galvin, Wat (high sticking), 4:12; Falite, Wat (roughing), 4:12; Brett MacKinnon, CR (holding), 5:02; Snavely, CR (hooking), 5:51; Fulghum, Wat (unsportsmanlike conduct), 5:51; Lalande, CR (interference), 7:30; Johnson, CR (high sticking), 8:44; Grubb, Wat (roughing), 8:44; Rob Hammel, Wat (roughing) 13:54; bench minor, CR (too many men), 15:15.

Third Period – 6, Cedar Rapids, Danny O'Brien (Patton, Dave Moss), 12:19 (pp). 7, Cedar Rapids, Hickey (Patton), 17:45. Penalties – Velebny, Wat (tripping), 1:27; Fulghum, Wat (roughing), 3:32; Grubb, Wat (slashing), 3:32; David Carpenter, CR (roughing), 3:32; Carpenter, CR (slashing), 3:32; Grubb, Wat (holding), 8:51; Falite, Wat (roughing), 9:59; Darren Partch, CR (unsportsmanlike conduct), 9:59; bench minor, Wat (too many men), 12:03; Daramy, CR (delay of game), 19:56; Velebny, Wat (delay of game), 19:56.

Shots on goal – Cedar Rapids 6-13-15 34. Waterloo 18-12-10 40.

Goalies – Cedar Rapids, Bobby Goepfert (40-37); Waterloo Adam Hanna (34-30).

Attendance – 3,175.

2001
Cedar Rapids RoughRiders 7, Black Hawks 0

The Teddy Bear Toss was conceived in Canada during the early 1990s. The idea had been implemented in many other junior and minor league cities long before it came to the Cedar Valley. Tens of thousands of plush toys had already been thrown onto the ice at rinks across the continent before the first bear was flipped over Young Arena's glass. Yet for Waterloo fans, it was easy to establish the Teddy Bear Toss tradition when it became a part of the traditional Thanksgiving experience.

The new toys collected by the Black Hawks each year are mainly donated to Toys for Tots and other comparable organizations. Some are gifted to kids directly when the team interacts with children for skating events and other activities. There are fans who try to bring the biggest bear (occasionally too big for a seat) or the most unique toy, but all are appreciated when they find their way to their future home. For a few moments, the game stops for a metaphorical shower of love and good fellowship.

But the Teddy Bear Toss should begin with Waterloo's first goal.

Before the 2001 Thanksgiving game, the Hawks had already been shutout five times that fall, including six scoreless periods against the Cedar Rapids RoughRiders. During 3-0 and 6-0 results, Bobby Goepfert had totaled 73 saves. His shutouts versus Waterloo were part of a season in which he would record eight. The first of several remarkable Cedar Rapids netminders, Goepfert appeared in all but 10 of the RoughRiders' games that winter. He was named the USHL Goaltender of the Year and drafted by the Pittsburgh Penguins in June of 2002.

Goepfert and his Cedar Rapids teammates came to Young Arena as the first place team in the East Division with an 11-4-1 record. During the opening 20 minutes, Cedar Rapids only needed him to make five saves against the last place Hawks. He did it, and Danny O'Brien – who had played a significant role in the 2000 Thanksgiving game – stuffed in the opening goal. Nate Meyers also found the net, then did so again in the visitors' two-goal second period. Goepfert made eight more saves, and by the second intermission, it was 4-0.

When asked about his favorite movie in a Cedar Rapids questionnaire, Bobby Goepfert picked the 1952 western High Noon. *It was an appropriate choice for a player fully capable of winning any goaltending duel.*

"The chances we had weren't great compared to theirs," conceded Coach Scott Koberinski. "We don't have any extra drive to score. We don't have the extra drive to stop anybody. It all comes down to, 'Do you really care?' and right now it seems like we don't."

There was no third period tension about whether the Black Hawks would rally to contest the inescapable outcome. Less than three minutes after intermission, Cedar Rapids made it 5-0. One lingering question was settled at 6:37 when Meyers completed his hat trick. Whether Goepfert would earn another shutout, and the fate of hundreds of teddy bears, were the last points of interest as the night wound down.

Goepfert did finish off Waterloo with a 23-save performance. Cedar Rapids' fifth successful penalty kill concluded with under five minutes to play and perhaps provided the Hawks with their last substantial opportunity to break the Long Island goaltender's spell.

The Black Hawks' first Thanksgiving Teddy Bear Toss was unique. It happened after the game was over.

Cedar Rapids   2 2 3 – 7
Waterloo   0 0 0 – 0

First Period – 1, Cedar Rapids, Danny O'Brien (Nate Meyers, Todd Bentley), 8:56. 2, Cedar Rapids, Meyers (Stephen Burgess), 16:23. Penalties – Ryan Langenbrunner, Wat (Slashing), 2:27; Burgess, CR (delay of game), 8:10; Greg Poupard, Wat (delay of game), 8:10; P.J. Atherton, CR (hooking), 10:05; Eric Weum, Wat (holding) 10:59; Nick Toneys, Wat (roughing), 16:38; Meyers, CR (interference), 18:15.

Second Period – 3, Cedar Rapids, Bentley (Atherton), 2:36; 4, Cedar Rapids, Meyers (Joe Gasparini, Ted O'Leary), 6:37 (pp). Penalties – Jake Schwan, Wat (slashing), 6:26; Chase Watson, CR (roughing), 9:47; Poupard, Wat (roughing), 9:47; Ben Mettler, Wat (delay of game), 10:34; Burgess, CR (delay of game), 10:34; O'Brien, CR (roughing double minor), 19:54; Dan Krmpotich, Wat (roughing), 19:54.

Third Period – 5, Cedar Rapids, Ryan Webb (Watson), 2:11. 6, Cedar Rapids, Meyers (Bentley, O'Brien), 5:47. 7, Cedar Rapids, Bentley (Meyers, Tony Gill), 16:27. Penalties – Poupard, Wat (holding), 6:21; Kevin Brooks, CR (hooking), 8:49; Mettler, Wat (holding), 10:00; Jim Jensen, Wat (roughing) 12:43; Atherton, CR (holding), 13:54.

Shots on goal – Cedar Rapids 9-9-8 26. Waterloo 5-8-10 23.

Goalies – Cedar Rapids, Bobby Goepfert (23-23); Waterloo, Josh Siembida (12-8), Kyle McNulty (14-11).

Attendance – 2,659.

2002
Black Hawks 5, Cedar Rapids RoughRiders 4 (SO)

Black Hawks players and fans didn't realize it then, but late November games in 2002 were part of the longest winning streak in franchise history up to that time. P.K. O'Handley's first Waterloo squad had a tepid first six weeks, which quickly turned torrid thereafter. By the middle of December, the Hawks won 12 consecutive games.

Years later, Captain Trevor Stewart talked about the differences between his first and second seasons playing at Young Arena.

"The Black Hawks changed overnight when Coach O'Handley was hired. He immediately had the respect of his players and the Waterloo community. Coach O'Handley developed a culture that made it a tremendous privilege to throw on a Black Hawks sweater."

By Thanksgiving week, the Hawks had pulled themselves above .500. A win in Cedar Rapids the night before the holiday put Waterloo at 10-8-1. It also brought the division-leading RoughRiders (11-7-3) almost within striking distance.

The 2002 Teddy Bear Toss was far different than the previous year's experience; it was touched off by a pair of veterans who had been on hand for the 2001 shutout. Just 2:27 into the first period, Joel Hanson sprang Mike Dagenais up the ice alone. The Waterloo forward beat 6-foot-3-inch Cedar Rapids goalie Joe Fallon to stir the crowd of 3,200 and bring a volley of toys to the ice. After Black Hawks interns and Young Arena staff scrambled to clear the stuffed animals, the rest of the period was played with no change in score.

Waterloo worked quickly at the start of a more offensive second period. Like Stewart, Hanson, and Dagenais, Ross Carlson had been with the club long enough to appreciate the before-and-after experience which came with O'Handley's arrival. Carlson's unassisted breakaway goal made it 2-0 at 1:32.

However, the Hawks could not pull away farther. Cedar Rapids' third power play of the night produced a goal at 5:32. Then Joe Pavelski notched his ninth of the season by following up on a Derek Whitmore shot which had been stopped. Yet the RoughRiders pulled even before intermission on two goals scored in less two minutes.

Whitmore produced a go-ahead tally at 4:55 of the third. This time Pavelski helped create the play with Jim Jensen. The 4-3 score held until there were less than two minutes remaining.

"It was good to get out to the early lead, but we made a mistake in regulation which forced overtime," O'Handley conceded.

That mistake was a turnover, which allowed the RoughRiders' Derek Peltier to notch his third point of the night, following a pair of earlier assists. Peltier's game-tying goal at 18:14 was one of only two Cedar Rapids shots during the period.

The Hawks out-chanced their guests 4-1 in the overtime, but with no scoring, the 32nd Thanksgiving game played in Waterloo became the first to be settled in a shootout. Fallon and Hawks goalie Jeff Jakaitis each started well, before Matt Fornataro – the youngest Black Hawks forward – pushed Waterloo ahead with a conversion in the third round. Jakaitis did the rest to claim the five-round shootout, 1-0.

Matt Fornataro scored just once in his first 15 Black Hawks games. However, he had goals in each of the two games prior to Thanksgiving and was heating up to notch a total of 15 in 2002/03.

Overall it was Waterloo's seventh consecutive win and also part of a longer string of victories on home ice. Beginning November 2nd and running through January 24th – a span of 14 games – the Hawks didn't lose at Young Arena.

Home success became a characteristic of O'Handley's teams, and the 2002/03 Black Hawks wound finish with a 25-3-2 record at the rink on Commercial Street.

Cedar Rapids   **0 3 1 0 0 – 4**
Waterloo   **1 2 1 0 1 – 5**

First Period – 1, Waterloo, Mike Dagenais (Joel Hanson), 2:27. Penalties – Rob Lehtinen, Wat (interference), 5:33; Matt Fornataro, Wat (hooking), 9:51; Zach Miskovic, CR (elbowing), 12:55.

Second Period – 2, Waterloo, Ross Carlson (unassisted), 1:32. 3, Cedar Rapids, Shawn Vinz (Kevin Brooks, Derek Peltier), 5:38 (pp). 4, Waterloo, Joe Pavelski (Derek Whitmore), 12:03. 5, Cedar Rapids, Jon Grabarek (unassisted), 15:46. 6, Cedar Rapids, Tyler Howells (Chase Watson, Peltier), 17:08. Penalties – Jake Schwan, Wat (slashing), 5:15; Brooks, CR (tripping), 17:26.

Third Period – 7, Waterloo, Whitmore (Jim Jensen, Pavelski), 4:55. 8, Cedar Rapids, Peltier (Vinz, Grabarek), 18:14. Penalties – Matt Olinger, CR (interference), :32; bench minor, Wat (too many men), 9:41; Miskovic, CR (tripping), 12:16; Fornataro, Wat (delay of game), 13:42; Lehtinen, Wat (high sticking), 13:42; Olinger, CR (delay of game), 13:42.

Overtime – no scoring. Penalties – none.

Shootout – Cedar Rapids, Troy Brummett (no goal), Zach Pearson (no goal), Howells (no goal), Watson (no goal), Brooks (no goal). Waterloo, Whitmore (no goal), Mike Radja (no goal), Fornataro (goal), Pavelski (no goal).

Shots on goal – Cedar Rapids 12-7-2-1-0 22. Waterloo 8-10-4-4-1 27.

Goalies – Cedar Rapids, Joe Fallon (26-22, shootout 4-3); Waterloo, Jeff Jakaitis (22-18; shootout, 5-5).

2003
Cedar Rapids RoughRiders 4, Black Hawks 2

The Thanksgiving game in Waterloo is a wonderful tradition for families. Many now think of it as something akin to the festive meal, the Detroit Lions, and the beginning of holiday shopping. For players, coaches, and officials, the experience offers a vibrant, lively atmosphere which is hard to capture outside of the playoffs. With all of Thanksgiving's virtues however, it should not be considered an omen for what will follow in the more-than three dozen games remaining on the schedule each season.

The 2003/04 Black Hawks were near their lowest point when Thanksgiving arrived. After a 4-0-0 start, Waterloo's record in the next 13 games was 2-10-1. One night earlier, the RoughRiders had beaten the Hawks 4-2. That loss was Waterloo's fourth-in-a-row, and in the process, Cedar Rapids earned their ninth consecutive win. The Hawks were last in the East Division, and the RoughRiders were first.

With those trends established, the game began almost exactly as might have been expected: just 16 seconds into the first period, the Hawks coughed up the puck, putting James Brannigan in position to score the fastest Thanksgiving goal since 1987. Waterloo went to a power play less than a minute later but did not answer. Instead, Cedar Rapids' Matt Vokes tallied the first special teams goal of the night during a five-on-three power play in the last minute before intermission.

The Hawks were able to swing themselves back into the game during the second period, thanks to a combination of success on the advantage and while shorthanded. First-year defenseman J.P. Testwuide had scored his first USHL goal less than a week earlier and drove the puck between the pipes again at 9:34 during a power play. Minutes later, the Hawks were penalty killing when Joel Hanson was able to force a takeaway and set up Joe Pavelski's shorthanded equalizer. Coincidentally, it was Pavelski's ninth goal of the season, as had been the case when he scored on Thanksgiving in 2002.

J.P. Testwuide (right) and his brother, Mike, each spent two seasons in Waterloo. Later they would play for rival NCAA programs: J.P. at Denver and Mike with Colorado College.

Unfortunately for Waterloo, mistakes in the third period nullified a 13-6 shots advantage. The first period goals by Brannigan and Vokes had been encores after each had scored in the Wednesday night meeting. Billy Loupee joined the group of RoughRiders who found the net in both games, capitalizing after a turnover at 3:46. He then outdid his two teammates seven minutes later when he scored again as the result of another Hawks mistake.

"When you're behind, you have to take chances to try to generate some offensive opportunities," conceded Coach P.K. O'Handley, "But every time you take a chance, you risk a turnover. And when you turn it over, the puck can end up in the net."

Joe Fallon stopped all of Waterloo's third period chances and made 30 total saves to level his Thanksgiving record at 1-1. The Cedar Rapids holiday week sweep gave the RoughRiders three victories in five 2003/04 meetings with the Hawks.

The teams did not face each other again until February and March; the Hawks won each of the three contests during that portion of the schedule. Those favorable results were vital to Waterloo's bid for a postseason berth, while the RoughRiders came up one point short of winning the division. In the playoffs which followed, Cedar Rapids was eliminated in the first round; the Hawks surprised the Chicago Steel and then the rest of the USHL. From the depths of the standings at Thanksgiving, Waterloo went on to win the Clark Cup, the team's first championship in 25 years.

Cedar Rapids   2 0 2 – 4
Waterloo   0 2 0 – 2

First Period – 1, Cedar Rapids, James Brannigan (Derek Peltier, Jon Grabarek), :16. 2, Cedar Rapids, Matt Vokes (Jamie Carroll), 19:08 (pp). Penalties – Bryan Horan, CR (hooking), 1:11; Andrew Guyer, Wat (hooking), 8:34; Mike Radja, Wat (roughing), 15:33; Brett Beckfeld, CR (roughing), 15:33; Tim Madsen, Wat (holding), 17:30; Andrew Thomas, Wat (holding), 18:37.

Second Period – 3, Waterloo, J.P. Testwuide (Madsen, Radja), 9:34 (pp). 4, Waterloo, Joe Pavelski (Joel Hanson), 12:09 (sh). Penalties – Derek Peltier, CR (tripping), 1:38; Greg Collins, CR (boarding), 8:18; Zach Bearson, Wat (tripping), 11:42.

Third Period – 5, Cedar Rapids, Billy Loupee (Horan), 3:46. 6, Cedar Rapids, Loupee (Sean Muncy, Jordan Hart), 10:44. Penalties – John Vadnais, Wat (cross checking), 6:54; Peltier, CR (roughing), 6:54; Carroll, CR (hooking), 13:12; David Meckler, Wat (tripping), 16:41.

Shots on goal – Cedar Rapids 11-4-6 21. Waterloo 11-8-13 32.

Goalies – Cedar Rapids, Joe Fallon (32-30); Waterloo, Kevin Regan (21-17).

Attendance – 3,194.

2004
Cedar Rapids RoughRiders 2, Black Hawks 1 (SO)

P.K. O'Handley has coached the Black Hawks in 18 of the team's first 50 Thanksgiving games, and before that, he led the North Iowa Huskies into two others. The former psychology student knows that after the game, the participants reflect warmly on the experience. Yet the time leading up to the first faceoff often comes with a different emotion.

"To a young guy, it's difficult, and if their parents aren't here, it's more difficult, because it's potentially the first major holiday that they weren't with family. It's tough on the players of both teams during the day, and then you get out in the environment, and it's one of the better environments that the players on both teams will play in in their entire careers. After you've been through it as a player, I think you anticipate the excitement."

The experience for a rookie is foreshadowed long before game day. In the weeks ahead of the holiday, the veterans share their stories of the experience. Their enthusiasm typically breaks through on some level, but hearing about the game – whether as a player, coach, or fan – doesn't compare with firsthand familiarity.

In 2004, both clubs sent first-year goalies to the crease. Alex Stalock had opened the season 6-3-1 for Cedar Rapids. Although his save percentage was just over .900 at the time, Stalock's performance as the RoughRiders went on to earn the Clark Cup would lead the San Jose Sharks to draft him in the fourth round the next summer. As of late November however, the Hawks' Drew O'Connell was earning better results. O'Connell was stopping the puck at a .937 rate and owned two shutouts as part of his 5-2-1 record.

"There wasn't a more fun atmosphere to play in than when Young Arena was packed and the fans were raucous," remembered O'Connell later. "Learning to deal with pressure situations was something I took from

Waterloo…[It] really prepared me to handle difficult situations better."

Neither netminder could be beaten for most of the first period, but the Hawks benefitted from a timely bounce during a power play. Drew Dobson's initial chance flew wide of the goal with just under a minute remaining. It caromed off the end wall and found Jesse Vesel. Customarily a defenseman, Vesel was being used as a forward and made the most of his opportunity.

In the second, a Cedar Rapids power play produced the only regulation chance that eluded O'Connell. Matt Vokes – one of the 13 combined skaters who had played for one of the two clubs on Thanksgiving in 2003 – beat O'Connell with a shot that found the net. In the third, both goalies saw pucks which flew past them but struck iron and bounced away. O'Connell heard a ping over his shoulder in the first minute on an attempt by Rob Ricci, and Stalock had the same luck on Andy Bohmbach's chance to win the game with the last shot of regulation.

With overtime opportunities added to the total, O'Connell made 24 saves and Stalock had 29. Two future NHL'ers lined up for Cedar Rapids shootout attempts, and O'Connell denied one of them. Teddy Purcell converted the first opportunity of the tie-breaker, but Justin Abdelkader could not follow up in the third round. However, Purcell's chance was as good as a game-winner, because Stalock stopped everything. Cedar Rapids won the four-round shootout 2-0 to cap one of the best-balanced goaltending duels ever seen on the holiday.

After seven seasons with the North Iowa Huskies, then four years in the ECHL, O'Handley's time in Waterloo has provided the chance to set USHL records for wins and games coached.

Cedar Rapids   0 1 0 0 1 – 2
Waterloo   1 0 0 0 0 – 1

First Period – 1, Waterloo, Jesse Vesel (Drew Dobson, Andy Bohmbach), 19:07 (pp). Penalties – Scott Birnstill, Wat (roughing); Jordan Pietrus, CR (holding), 18:08.

Second Period – 2, Cedar Rapids, Matt Vokes (Shane Lovdahl, Phil Axtell), 8:13. Penalties – Nathan Lawrence, Wat (holding), 3:50; J.P. Testwuide, Wat (holding), 6:16; Tim Filangieri, Wat (delay of game), 6:16; Raymond Eichenlaub, CR (delay of game), 6:16; Testwuide, Wat (delay of game), 13:32; Eichenlaub, CR (interference), 13:32; Greg Collins, CR (delay of game), 13:32; Lawrence, Wat (high sticking), 16:44.

Third Period – no scoring. Penalties – Axtell, CR (roughing), 2:21; Matt Arhontas, Wat (tripping), 4:41; Dobson, Wat (holding), 7:19; Vokes, CR (unsportsmanlike conduct), 7:19; Michael Annett, Wat (high sticking), 7:54.

Overtime – no scoring. Penalties – none.

Shootout – Cedar Rapids, Ted Purcell (goal), Rob Ricci (no goal), Justin Abdelkader (no goal), Jon Grabarek (goal). Waterloo, Bohmbach (no goal), David Meckler (no goal), Vesel (no goal), Garrett Regan (no goal).

Shots on goal – Cedar Rapids 7-7-9-2-1 26. Waterloo 13-4-9-4-0 30.

Goalies – Cedar Rapids, Alex Stalock (30-29, shootout 4-4); Waterloo, Drew O'Connell (25-24; shootout, 4-2).

Attendance – 3,189.

2005
Black Hawks 5, Cedar Rapids RoughRiders 4

In 2002, 2003, and 2004, the Black Hawks and RoughRiders played a pre-Thanksgiving game one night earlier at Cedar Rapids Ice Arena. During each of those years, the team that won on Wednesday also picked up a victory on Thursday. The schedule followed the same pattern in 2005. During the first matchup of that holiday week, the RoughRiders came back from a 2-1 second intermission deficit on home ice, edging the Hawks 3-2 in overtime. Forward Phil Axtell scored the game-tying goal during a power play midway through the third period on an assist from Chad Costello.

In the rematch, the same two players were pivotal to a RoughRider comeback, but the Waterloo lead was much bigger.

A pair of veterans put the Hawks ahead in just 25 seconds. Captain Zach Bearson had the first look at Cedar Rapids netminder Alex Stalock; Matt Arhontas collected the puck for a second-chance score. It broke a nine-game goalless drought after the speedy fan-favorite had opened the year with five goals in the first six games.

The Hawks recorded two more tallies in the opening 20 minutes to a take a 3-0 lead to intermission. Defenseman Jacob Schuster had played for Cedar Rapids three years earlier; he scored his first goal for Waterloo during a power play at 6:10. The Hawks added a second special teams goal almost three minutes later when Mitch Ryan tipped a shot by Vince LoVerde.

Although the RoughRiders had a successful power play early in the second, the period turned into a stalemate, and Waterloo outshot the visitors 20-12. Mike Borisenok and Mike Testwuide made the score 5-1 before Cedar Rapids could inch any closer.

However, Axtell almost brought Cedar Rapids back again. Before the second intermission, Costello set him up between the circles for a power play goal. On the advantage again nearly six minutes into the third, the same combination clicked to make it a 5-3 game. Then Nick Sellers lifted in a backhander with 11:25 remaining, leaving the Hawks and their fans on edge with a one-goal margin. A second (and much bigger) Cedar Rapids comeback in two days seemed entirely possible.

Six of the nine combined goals during the game had been recorded on the power play, and the RoughRiders had a last special teams chance when Joe Sova was called for tripping at 12:04. However the Hawks were able to preserve the lead, leaving less than six minutes to go when Sova returned to action.

Joe Grossman made his biggest save of the night four minutes later, before Cedar Rapids pulled Stalock. With a pileup near the front of the net, the Hawks' goalie denied Kevin Wehrs, who had snuck in from his spot on the blue line to poke at the puck in the scrum.

Stalock made it to the bench with under a minute to go, but the RoughRiders didn't have enough time to tie it, nor did Arhontas have enough time for his second goal of the night when his attempted empty-netter crossed the goal line after regulation had ended. Instead, ten different Black Hawks were each credited with one point in the well-rounded win.

Don't be confused by the nickname; Matt "Pokey" Arhontas was one of Waterloo's speediest and feistiest players during his three seasons as a Black Hawk.

Cedar Rapids   0   2   2 – 4
Waterloo   3   2   0 – 5

First Period – 1, Waterloo, Matt Arhontas (Zach Bearson), :25. 2, Waterloo, Jacob Schuster (Cody Chupp), 6:10 (pp). 3, Waterloo, Mitch Ryan (Vince LoVerde), 8:51 (pp). Penalties – Chupp, Wat (holding), :35; Brett Dickinson,

CR (tripping), 5:39; Ted Purcell, CR (hooking), 6:57; Schuster, Wat (high sticking), 10:34; Schuster, Wat (roughing), 13:57; Scott Wietecha, CR (roughing), 13:57; Phil Axtell, CR (charging), 13:57.

Second Period – 4, Cedar Rapids, David Strathman (Chad Costello, Ted Purcell), 6:12 (pp). 5, Waterloo, Mike Borisenok (Kyle Reeds), 8:18. 6, Waterloo, Mike Testwuide (Garrett Suter), 12:23 (pp). 7, Cedar Rapids, Axtell (Costello, Purcell), 16:15 (pp). Penalties – Suter, Wat (holding), 4:23; Tim Gilbert, Wat (delay of game), 9:14; Kevin Wehrs, CR (delay of game), 9:14; Christian Jensen, Wat (holding), 9:25; Drew Dobson, Wat (roughing), 11:15; Gary Steffes, CR (roughing), 11:15; Nick Grasso, CR (boarding), 11:15; Andy Bohmbach, Wat (delay of game), 11:46; Steven Kaunisto, CR (delay of game), 11:46; Gilbert, Wat (fighting), 14:30; Ray Kaunisto, CR (fighting), 14:30; Schuster, Wat (roughing), 15:36; Andy Miele, CR (slashing), 19:43.

Third Period – 8, Cedar Rapids, Axtell (Costello, S. Kaunisto), 5:47 (pp). 8, Cedar Rapids, Nik Sellers (Wietecha), 8:35. Penalties – Joe Sova, Wat (tripping), 4:54; Sova, Wat (tripping), 12:04.

Shots on goal – Cedar Rapids 5-12-8 25. Waterloo 13-20-7 40.

Goalies – Cedar Rapids, Alex Stalock (40-35); Waterloo, Joe Grossman (25-21).

Attendance – 3,314.

2006
Cedar Rapids RoughRiders 3, Black Hawks 2

As the Black Hawks' Thanksgiving contest became a fixture on the annual schedule during the 1970s and 80s, Waterloo's opponents for the game changed with regularity. In the 1980s, the Hawks faced the Des Moines Buccaneers in four consecutive years and six times during the decade. In 2006, Waterloo met the Cedar Rapids RoughRiders for the seventh consecutive time, more than any other opponent on the holiday, whether in sequential years or otherwise.

The RoughRiders had relocated from Mason City and rebranded in 1999 when owner Butch Johnson (also then owner of the Black Hawks) made a major investment in Cedar Rapids Ice Arena and convinced city officials there to meet him part way to fund the facility. Although they missed the playoffs in their first season, the RoughRiders wouldn't be held out again for more than a decade. They won a share of the Anderson Cup in 2004/05, then earned the Clark Cup that spring. It all happened under the direction of Head Coach Mark Carlson.

However, Carlson's first impression of Thanksgiving hockey in Waterloo predated bringing his own team to the rink.

"When I was in college hockey, I was here for at least one [Thanksgiving game]," Carlson recalled, "...it's become a way of life for me and quite honestly, I feel fortunate to be a part of it."

In the 2006 matchup, Carlson's team took the lead when Jacob Cepis scored his 11th goal of the season at 15:25. The 18-year-old was in his second year with the RoughRiders after previously playing closer to home with the Cleveland Barons in the North American Hockey League. Going on to lead the USHL with 34 goals in 2006/07, Cepis' college career would later mirror his time at the junior level: two years in his home state at Bowling Green before finishing as a rare out-of-stater at the University of Minnesota while he was an upperclassman.

Waterloo's Jan-Mikael Juutilainen tied the game on an unassisted goal with 23 seconds remaining before intermission. Juutilainen had been drafted that summer by the Chicago Blackhawks and spent the next two years trying to adjust to the North American game and lifestyle in Waterloo. His Thanksgiving equalizer came when he stole a puck at the RoughRider blue line, then blasted it by goalie Richard Bachman from the top of the left circle.

Jan-Mikael Juutilainen was the first player to be both drafted by the Chicago Blackhawks and play for the Waterloo Black Hawks.

Cedar Rapids swung back to the lead in the first minute of the second period on a shot by Scott Wietecha. Then at 6:05 of the third period, Cepis scored his second of the night in similar fashion to Juutilainen's goal. Finding a loose puck at center, Cepis made it a 3-1 game with an unassisted breakaway backhander.

Meanwhile, Waterloo's power play largely faltered against an opponent that was killing off just over 80 percent of opposing chances. Midway through the third, the Hawks' ninth and tenth power plays of the game overlapped. Just as the first RoughRider penalty was ending, Juutilainen notched his second goal of the night, but the Hawks could not tie it during the remaining five-on-four time, nor on another later power play, finishing one-for-11 on the advantage.

After suffering their first home ice loss of the season, Waterloo would recover and win in Cedar Rapids the next night. Another victory there during the final game of the regular season gave the Hawks the Anderson Cup. It also made 2006/07 the fourth time in five years that either the Hawks or

RoughRiders had won at least a share of the East Division and the third time in that span that they had finished first and second together.

Cedar Rapids   **1 1 1 – 3**
Waterloo   **1 0 1 – 2**

First Period – 1, Cedar Rapids, Jacob Cepis (Rob Bordson), 15:25. 2, Waterloo, Jan-Mikael Juutilainen (unassisted), 19:37. Penalties – Evan Stephens, CR (high sticking), 4:38; Tim Gilbert, Wat (high sticking), 7:25; bench minor, CR (too many men), 8:57; Sergei Kolosov, CR (hooking), 19:48.

Second Period – 3, Cedar Rapids, Scott Wietecha (David Boehm, Robin Bergman), :54 (pp). Penalties – Wietecha, CR (holding), 2:44; Gilbert, Wat (interference), 5:48; James Marcou, Wat (tripping), 8:13; Pasko Skarica, Wat (hooking), 10:39; Stephens, CR (interference), 18:51.

Third Period – 4, Cedar Rapids, Cepis (unassisted), 6:05. 5, Waterloo, Juutilainen (Brett Barta, Blake Kessel), 10:58 (pp). Penalties – Brett Dickinson, CR (interference), 1:42; Dickinson, CR (holding) 3:57; Isak Tranvik, Wat (delay of game), 5:37; Stephens, CR (delay of game), 5:37; Mike Seidel, CR (checking from behind), 6:52; Juutilainen, Wat (holding), 8:13; Dickinson, CR (tripping), 8:59; Kevin Wehrs, CR (cross checking), 9:58; Tranvik, Wat (cross checking), 12:32; Scott Mathis, CR (hooking), 15:08.

Shots on goal – Cedar Rapids 8-12-4 24. Waterloo 9-13-9 31.

Goalies – Cedar Rapids, Richard Bachman (31-29); Waterloo – Matt DiGirolamo (24-21).

Attendance – 3,500.

2007
Cedar Rapids RoughRiders 2, Black Hawks 1 (SO)

When the RoughRiders and Black Hawks met on November's fourth Thursday in 2007, Cedar Rapids hoped to jump past the Indiana Ice into first place in the USHL East Division. Waterloo was a regulation win away from tying the RoughRiders for second place. The Hawks were the defending Anderson Cup Champions and had won seven consecutive games. Cedar Rapids stayed ahead of the streaking Hawks, thanks in part to 17-year-old goaltender Brady Hjelle.

The RoughRiders might have expected veteran Kent Patterson to be their starting netminder, but due to injury, Patterson had not yet played by that point in the regular season. As a result, Hjelle had appeared in all but two games and accumulated a league-leading nine wins. Waterloo had barely scratched out a 3-2 shootout victory against him three weeks earlier at Cedar Rapids Ice Arena.

The earlier meeting had gone to overtime thanks to a game-tying goal by Black Hawks defenseman Drew MacKenzie. The Buffalo Sabres draft pick was notably involved again right away on Thanksgiving. Just more than a minute after puck drop, MacKenzie dropped his gloves with Cedar Rapids veteran Tyler Thompson. The fight came while many in the crowd of 3,500 were still navigating toward their seats.

Defensemen were responsible for all of the scoring in regulation. At 12:06 of the first period, Cedar Rapids' Scott Mathis fired in a shot from above the left circle, and the Hawks trailed at intermission despite outshooting the RoughRiders 12-7. Chances weighed even more heavily toward Waterloo in the second, but Hjelle stopped everything except a five-on-three power play opportunity. Seconds after the two-man advantage began, Blake Kessel lifted the puck to the top corner to knot up the score.

Not to be overshadowed by his famous brother (Phil) or sister (Amanda), Blake Kessel was an All-American at New Hampshire after being the USHL Defenseman of the Year in 2007/08.

The game was still tied late in regulation when the RoughRiders were presented with a prime opportunity to lock up their sixth Thanksgiving win. With 3:25 to go, Hawks forward Billy Maday was given a four minute checking from behind penalty. Waterloo scrambled through the shorthanded situation to reach overtime and earn one standings point. The power play helped Cedar Rapids outshoot the Hawks 11-10 in the third, the only period in which they had an edge.

A scoreless overtime put Waterloo in a seemingly good circumstance; the Hawks were 4-0 in shootouts and had converted nine of their 24 attempts in the first two months of the schedule. At that time, USHL shootouts were five rounds, unless one team had an insurmountable advantage. Hjelle beat the first four Waterloo attempts. Only Jan-Mikael Juutilainen's goal in the fifth round extended the game; Garrett Vermeersch had pushed the RoughRiders ahead on their fourth try. Cedar Rapids' Ian Slater scored right after Juutilainen, and Hjelle stopped one more Waterloo attempt to claim the win. Before denying five of six Hawks shootout tries, Hjelle had turned away 37 of 38 shots in regulation and overtime.

Cedar Rapids and Waterloo would go to overtime in four of their eight meetings during 2007/08 and once in a playoff series which followed. The Thanksgiving shootout was the only overtime against the RoughRiders that winter which didn't break the Hawks' way.

Cedar Rapids   1 0 0 0 1 – 2
Waterloo   0 1 0 0 0 – 1

First Period – 1, Cedar Rapids, Scott Mathis (David Boehm, Kyle Flanagan), 12:06. Penalties – Drew MacKenzie, Wat (fighting), 1:07; Tyler Thompson, CR (fighting), 1:07; Mike Fink, Wat (interference), 2:37; Ben Lynch, CR (hooking), 4:29; Boehm, CR (slashing), 12:42; Paul Phillips, CR (hooking), 17:50.

Second Period – 2, Waterloo, Blake Kessel (Brett Olson, MacKenzie), 13:10 (pp). Penalties – Boehm, CR (hooking), 1:05; Phillips, CR (slashing), 7:34; Nick Larson, Wat (hooking), 9:52; Matt Tomassoni, CR (holding), 11:55; Chris Wideman, CR (cross checking), 13:04.

Third Period – no scoring. Penalties – MacKenzie, Wat (holding), 9:55; Billy Maday, Wat (checking from behind double minor), 16:35; Maday, Wat (game ejection), 16:35.

Overtime – no scoring. Penalties – none.

Shootout – Cedar Rapids, Lynch (no goal), Flanagan (no goal), Thompson (no goal), Garrett Vermeersch (goal), Casey Wellman (no goal), Ian Slater (goal). Waterloo, Fink (no goal), Scott Pavelski (no goal), Craig Smith (no goal), Olson (no goal), Jan-Mikael Juutilainen (goal), Siim Liivik (no goal).

Shots on goal – Cedar Rapids 7-5-11-2-1 26. Waterloo 12-13-10-3-0 38.

Goalies – Cedar Rapids, Brady Hjelle (38-37, shootout 6-5); Waterloo, Matt DiGirolamo (25-24; shootout, 6-4).

Attendance – 3,500.

2008
Black Hawks 5, Cedar Rapids RoughRiders 4

The Black Hawks were on the short side of the annual Thanksgiving game six of the first eight times they played the RoughRiders, but 2008 represented the beginning of Waterloo's longest winning streak to date in the annual holiday game. The evening's result was achieved even though the day started badly for goaltender Joe Howe.

"I got in a car accident driving home from morning skate; my dad was pretty upset with me," Howe remembered. "I ended up playing really well and was blown away by the electric atmosphere inside of Young Arena. I don't know if I've had chills like that for a long time. We won, and my dad wasn't quite as mad, but he still wasn't happy."

Howe and teammates Nick Larson, Craig Smith, and Lee Moffie had an uncharacteristic degree of familiarity with several opponents. All four had played for Mark Carlson, and with four of his players (Matt Donovan, Greg Burke, Nick Oddo, and Darren Rowe), earlier that month, winning a gold medal together for the United States at the World Junior A Challenge.

The Thanksgiving reunion was Waterloo's eighth victory in a row at home to open the 2008/09 schedule, the longest streak to begin a season since the Hawks had moved to Young Arena. It surpassed a similar run of seven straight, which the RoughRiders had halted on Thanksgiving in 2006. Earning the win was difficult, despite Eriah Hayes tipping in George Hughes' shot for the first goal 45 seconds into the game. Little else went right for most of the first two periods.

Cedar Rapids tied the score on Donovan's goal at 8:29, with one second remaining during a power play. Early in the second, a turnover forced the Hawks' Ryan Hill to yank Jeff Costello to the ice, preventing the Cedar Rapids forward's breakaway opportunity. Costello converted the resulting penalty shot. Donovan scored another power play goal in the second, and early in the third, Mike Seidel capitalized while the RoughRiders had a two-man advantage.

"...Way too many penalties," Hawks Coach P.K. O'Handley said afterwards. "Just stupid penalties. There is no other word for some of the penalties we took but stupid."

With Ben Miller's second period goal mixed in, Waterloo trailed 4-2 and had already scored more than a typical Cedar Rapids' opponent. The RoughRiders came into the evening allowing 1.8 goals against per game.

The Hawks' comeback started when Larson swept a rebound into a gaping net with 11:28 to go. Cedar Rapids held on to a 4-3 edge until Jordan Samuels-Thomas tied the game on a drive from the high slot with just over five minutes to play. Less than a minute after that, Larson won an offensive zone faceoff back to Derek Arnold. The puck wouldn't lie flat, but Arnold sent it toward the net. RoughRider goalie Mike Johnson – owner of the league's best save percentage and goals-against average to that point in the season – couldn't read the wobbling shot. The puck found its way home, and the last of three unanswered Waterloo goals proved to be the game-winner.

Being a goalie provides a lifetime of highs and lows. Perhaps that helped Joe Howe get through a day that was rough long before the puck dropped.

Howe finished with 21 saves and did not allow a RoughRider goal while the teams skated at even-strength. His three teammates who participated in the World Junior A Challenge each contributed at least one Thanksgiving point.

Cedar Rapids   1 2 1 – 4
Waterloo   1 1 3 – 5

First Period – 1, Waterloo, Eriah Hayes (George Hughes, Keegan Meuer), :45. 2, Cedar Rapids, Matt Donovan (Kyle Flanagan, Zach Lehrke), 8:29 (pp). Penalties – Scott Winkler, CR (hooking), 3:01; Mike Seidel, CR (slashing), 4:40; Eddie Olczyk, Wat (slashing), 6:30; Patrick Way, Wat (holding), 11:51; Paul Phillips, CR (tripping), 19:10.

Second Period – 3, Jeff Costello (penalty shot), 4:02. 4, Waterloo, Ben Miller (Olczyk, Lee Moffie), 7:56. 5, Cedar Rapids, Donovan (Winkler, Seidel), 10:03 (pp). Penalties – Eric Robinson, CR (roughing) 5:43; Doug Leaverton, CR (hooking), 8:21; Olczyk, Wat (hooking), 8:38; Moffie, Wat (interference), 9:17; Ben Lynch, CR (tripping), 14:18.

Third Period – 6, Cedar Rapids, Seidel (Winkler, Donovan), 2:07 (pp). 7, Waterloo, Nick Larson (Keegan Meuer, Derek Arnold), 8:32. 8, Waterloo, Jordan Samuels-Thomas (Craig Smith, Moffie), 14:55. 9, Waterloo, Arnold (Larson), 15:49. Penalties – Larson, Wat (unsportsmanlike conduct), 1:36; Brock Montpetit, Wat (high sticking), 2:07.

Shots on goal – Cedar Rapids 11-8-6 25. Waterloo 6-12-9 27.

Goalies – Cedar Rapids, Mike Johnson (27-22); Waterloo, Joe Howe (25-21).

Attendance – 3,500.

2009
Black Hawks 6, Cedar Rapids RoughRiders 3

As the 2009/10 season began, the United States Hockey League started using four officials on a limited basis. Each club could expect a second referee to take the ice for three home and three road games over the course of the year. Waterloo's first game under the plan was on Thanksgiving, with Boone Bruggman and Ken Anderson responsible for calling the penalties, while Dan Cohen and Shaun Morgan monitored for offsides and icing. With a capacity crowd at Young Arena for a rivalry game, the crew in stripes had a very active holiday evening.

Patrick Divjak was whistled for the first penalty – hooking – only 1:47 into the game. Waterloo turned aside the RoughRider power play and took the lead at 8:54. Veteran defenseman Dan Sova's shot from the left point handcuffed goalie Troy Grosenick and went between the pipes off the netminder's glove. Although that goal was scored five-on-five, very little of what remained in the first period would be played that way.

Waterloo went to the first power play of the sequence, which yielded only a brilliant glove save by C.J. Motte on Eric Robinson's shorthanded breakaway. With Sova sent to the penalty box shortly after that stop, Bryce Aneloski tied the game while the teams were four-on-four. Motte took a measure of revenge two minutes later, assisting on Brock Montpetit's transitional power play chance which caught Grosenick leaning the wrong direction. The heavy emphasis on special teams carried into the closing seconds; the Hawks were two-men shorthanded when Sova found control of the puck deep in his own zone, firing it off the glass and out to center. The first Hawks penalty to Montpetit was just expiring, and Sova's clear turned into an on-target pass, springing the Black Hawk captain on a shorthanded breakaway. Despite being tangled by a scrambling Cedar Rapids player, Montpetit's shot still found its way across the goal line to give the Hawks a 3-1 lead.

At the end of 20 minutes, Waterloo was one-for-two on the power play and four-for-four on the penalty kill.

Big Dan Sova had a goal, an assist, and was +4 during his second Thanksgiving appearance for Waterloo.

Cedar Rapids did break through for a special teams goal by Jayson Megna, followed immediately by a fracas which led to more penalties seven minutes into the second. However, the rest of the scoring was done at even strength: Divjak and Tyler Barnes each snapped four-game goalless streaks 33 seconds apart. True to form, each team was down one skater as the second period ended, with the Hawks and RoughRiders combining to incur 13 minor penalties by that time.

With the top lines and leading penalty killers burning through a lot of shifts, chances were limited in the third. The Hawks were held to a half dozen shots on goal, while the RoughRiders had just four, with their only goal coming from Peter Sakaris near the five-minute mark. Divjak scored his second of the evening with nine minutes to play. Finishing the night on-theme, Waterloo's Scott Wamsganz was in the penalty box when regulation expired.

Each team recorded one power play goal; the RoughRiders' came on nine opportunities, while the Black Hawks had five.

Cedar Rapids   1 1 1 – 3
Waterloo   3 2 1 – 6

First Period – 1, Waterloo, Dan Sova (J.T. Brown, Tyler Barnes), 8:54. 2,

Cedar Rapids, Bryce Aneloski (Zach Lehrke), 13:25. 3, Waterloo, Brock Montpetit (Derek Arnold, C.J. Motte), 15:28 (pp). 4, Waterloo, Montpetit (Sova, Zach Palmquist) 19:27 (sh). Penalties – Patrick Divjak, Wat (hooking), 1:47; Derek DeBlois, CR (hooking), 11:49; Sova, Wat (interference), 12:40; Justin Kovacs, CR (hooking), 14:24; Montpetit, Wat (hooking), 17:20; Blake Thompson, Wat (cross checking), 18:59.

Second Period – 5, Cedar Rapids, Jayson Megna (Lehrke, Jeff Costello), 7:06 (pp). 6, Waterloo, Divjak (Scott Wamsganz, Tyler Zepeda), 16:17. 7, Waterloo, Barnes (Montpetit, Palmquist), 16:50. Penalties – Tony Turgeon, Wat (holding), 2:23; Turgeon, Wat (boarding), 6:47; Motte, Wat (crossing red line), 7:06; Costello, CR (charging), 7:06; Aneloski, CR (interference), 12:41; Divjak, Wat (holding), 18:31; Eric Robinson, CR (tripping), 19:27.

Third Period – 8, Cedar Rapids, Peter Sakaris (Stu Wilson, Jordan DiGiando), 4:58. 9, Waterloo, Divjak (Cody von Rueden, Jamie Hill), 10:57. Penalties – Brown, Wat (tripping), 8:20; DeBlois, CR (holding), 14:29; Turgeon, Wat (delay of game), 17:00; Michael Parks, CR (delay of game), 17:00; Wamsganz (checking from behind), 18:15.

Shots on goal – Cedar Rapids 11-12-4 27. Waterloo 10-11-6 27.

Goalies – Cedar Rapids, Troy Grosenick (25-19), Matt Hemingway (2-2); Waterloo, Motte (27-24).

Attendance – 3,500.

2010
Black Hawks 3, Cedar Rapids RoughRiders 2 (OT)

When the Black Hawks walked out of the Resch Center in Green Bay after a 4-2 loss on the Wednesday before Thanksgiving, a north wind had started to whip the wet falling snow. Cautiously, the team bus rolled south on U.S. 41. It seemed to be taking an inordinate amount of time to reach the turnoff near Oshkosh. Then someone near the front realized what had happened: with snow pasted onto the road signs, the Hawks had passed their exit, rolled by Fond du Lac, and were well on their way to Milwaukee. The players tried to sleep as the bus wound through Wisconsin backroads and arrived home two hours later than expected.

Fittingly, a wintry trip which required the Hawks' bus to work overtime was the preface for a Thanksgiving game which went beyond regulation, once the Hawks arrived back at the rink later Thursday.

Meanwhile, the RoughRiders had cruised to an easy Thanksgiving Eve win at home versus the Sioux City Musketeers. They came to Waterloo after victories in eight of their previous ten games and with an 8-2-0 road record, including a season-opening win at Young Arena. Eleven minutes into the Thursday game, Cedar Rapids pulled ahead when Jayson Megna scored to cap an odd man rush.

The Hawks tied it in transition early in the second. The puck was kicked to neutral territory and found Jamie Hill for a breakaway. Skating in alone against Brady Hjelle, Hill beat the league's future Goaltender of the Year to the glove side.

"One of our strengths is our speed," noted P.K. O'Handley, "I'm not sure we have a ton of maturity up in front, but I think when you get in a bit of a horse-race game where you're getting saves on the back end, I think it certainly is an advantage for us."

Well-rested Gunnar Hughes scored the go-ahead goal almost six minutes later. Hughes had not been on the ice in Green Bay the night before, missing out due to a suspension. Waiting in front of the Cedar Rapids net, he swatted in a puck bounding out of the corner. However, Cedar Rapids retied it with the game's only power play conversion later in the period, and the rest of regulation was played without any further scoring.

Throughout the early portion of the 2010/11 schedule, the Black Hawks had been dealing with injuries. During Thanksgiving week, Ryan Papa was the beneficiary of unexpected playing time off the Waterloo affiliate list and had scored his first USHL goal the night before in Green Bay. Against the RoughRiders, Papa found himself on the ice almost two minutes into overtime after Hjelle had already turned away one good Hawks chance to win the game. Vince Hinostroza sprang Papa toward the net from near the Cedar Rapids blue line.

Papa cut toward the netmouth around a defender and put a shot on goal. Hjelle made the save but couldn't control the puck, and the 5-foot-7-inch 16-year-old scooted to the edge of the crease, found his own rebound, and knocked in the overtime winner.

Due to a manufacturing error, one sleeve on the jersey which Ryan Papa wore as an affiliate showed "25" and the other was stitched with "52." After scoring the game-winning overtime goal on Thanksgiving, everyone knew who he was, even without a number. ©Stephanie Lyn Photography.

The Black Hawks came off the bench to mob Papa beside the boards. The

RoughRiders would go on to win the Anderson Cup, and Waterloo would barely qualify for the USHL's expanded-format playoffs, but on Thanksgiving, the Hawks had just cause for celebrating one of the most thrilling and unlikely finishes in the history of the holiday game.

Cedar Rapids   1 1 0 0 – 2
Waterloo   0 2 0 1 – 3

First Period – 1, Cedar Rapids, Jayson Megna (Justin Kovacs, Andy Simpson), 10:58. Penalties – Max Edson, Wat (slashing), 2:40; Tanner Pond, CR (checking from behind), 13:16; Gunnar Hughes, Wat (high sticking), 17:14.

Second Period – 2, Waterloo, Jamie Hill (Jake Youso, Zach Palmquist), 2:24. 3, Waterloo, Hughes (Tyson Fulton, Tyler Zepeda), 8:12. 4, Cedar Rapids, Sam Warning (Simpson, Thomas Fallen), 13:11 (pp). Penalties – Blake Thompson, Wat (hooking), Dan McNamara, Wat (kneeing), 17:41.

Third Period – no scoring. Penalties – Michael Parks, CR (hooking), :41; Palmquist, Wat (high sticking), 2:28; Steven Hensley, CR (holding), 9:29.

Overtime – 5, Waterloo, Ryan Papa (Vince Hinostroza, Jacob MacDonald), 1:54. Penalties – none.

Shots on goal – Cedar Rapids 10-8-8-0 26. Waterloo 10-15-12-3 40.

Goalies – Cedar Rapids, Brady Hjelle (40-37); Waterloo, C.J. Motte (26-24).

Attendance – 3,500.

2011
Black Hawks 8, Cedar Rapids RoughRiders 4

Waterloo and Cedar Rapids were on opposing trajectories in late November of 2011. The RoughRiders were winless in their prior four games, but three of those losses had been in overtime. In each case, they had been held to two goals or less. The Black Hawks were on a four-game winning streak. Two nights earlier, Waterloo had a season-best offensive night during an 8-4 road victory against the U.S. National Team Development Program Under-17s, although it was a game which was far closer than the final score suggested.

Relief and excitement mixed again for Waterloo on Thanksgiving.

Hawks captain Aaron Pearce was injured and out of the lineup, creating a place for affiliate forward Jake Horton. Less than three minutes into the game, Horton recorded his first USHL point, helping to set up defenseman Ian McCoshen for the opening goal during a rousing first period. Two days earlier, McCoshen had scored his first USHL goal against the NTDP.

It was 2-0 before the five minute mark; Taylor Cammarata added to the lead on a wraparound at 4:23. Then after killing off nearly six consecutive minutes of Cedar Rapids power play time, the Hawks scored twice more before intermission. Nifty passing between Cammarata and Matias Cleland left Scott McDonald with an open net for his first USHL goal. Waterloo capped the frame when Tony Cameranesi capitalized on a turnover near the RoughRider blue line and sent home a wrister from the high slot.

The apparent rout continued in the second. Vince Hinostroza redirected a pass into the Cedar Rapids net at 4:45, but 56 seconds later the RoughRiders' Andrew Oglevie finished a chance from close range. Waterloo extended the lead to five one more time at 9:02 during a power play, when Jamie Hill set up Joe Rehkamp at the top of the crease. Ahead 6-1 against an opponent with a recently-sputtering offense, it looked likely to be an easy night.

However, half of regulation still remained, and in half a period, the visitors were gamely making it competitive once again. Cedar Rapids cut into the margin at 13:12 with a goal from Greg Amlong, then won the period with 3.2 seconds remaining. Oglevie flipped in his second of the night as players from both sides scrambled at the edge of the crease.

The RoughRiders added to the tension even more in the early third when Tanner Pond won a faceoff and flipped in an unassisted goal at 1:57. Four minutes later, Cedar Rapids had a power play opportunity to cut the lead to one when Waterloo's Eddie Wittchow was called for boarding.

Like McCoshen in the first period, a Hawks defenseman scoring for the second time in three days provided a lift. While penalty killing, Cameranesi poked a puck free near the Waterloo blue line, creating a shorthanded breakaway for James Hansen. Hurrying up the rink and expecting a challenge from a RoughRider desperately trying to get back into the play, Hansen blistered a shot from the left circle past goalie Matt McNeely.

Teammates rush to celebrate with James Hansen after his crucial third period shorthanded goal. It was one of four times he scored during two seasons playing for Waterloo. ©Stephanie Lyn Photography.

"I saw an opening and I took it," Hansen explained. "I told myself, I didn't want the Rider guy to catch me and I didn't want to miss the net, so those are the two things I was thinking about, and luckily the shot went in."

The RoughRiders pulled McNeely early, and Cameranesi sealed the win with an empty-netter (his fourth point of the game) at 17:33.

Cedar Rapids 0 3 1 – 4
Waterloo   4 2 2 – 8

First Period – 1, Waterloo, Ian McCoshen (Jake Horton, Mike Huntebrinker), 2:57. 2, Waterloo, Taylor Cammarata (Mark Naclerio), 4:23. 3, Waterloo, Scott MacDonald (Matias Cleland, Cammarata), 15:12. 4, Waterloo, Tony Cameranesi (Trevor Owens), 18:26. Penalties – Eddie Wittchow, Wat (high sticking double minor), 4:55; McCoshen, Wat (high sticking), 8:48; Stu Wilson, CR (slashing), 12:45; Cleland, Wat (holding), 16:55; Tanner Pond, CR (unsportsmanlike conduct), 16:55.

Second Period – 5, Waterloo, Vince Hinostroza (Cameranesi), 4:45. 6, Cedar Rapids, Andrew Oglevie (Pond, Landon Smith), 5:41; 7, Waterloo, Joe Rehkamp (Jamie Hill, Mitch Witek), 8:25 (pp). 8, Cedar Rapids, Greg Amlong (Nick Saracino), 13:12. 9, Cedar Rapids, Oglevie (Pond), 19:57. Penalties – Amlong, CR (cross checking), 7:24; Hill, Wat (delay of game), 16:13; Ian Brady, CR (delay of game), 16:13.

Third Period – 10, Cedar Rapids, Pond (unassisted), 1:57. 11, Waterloo, James Hansen (Cameranesi, Hinostroza), 6:14 (sh). 12, Waterloo, Cameranesi (MacDonald), 17:33 (en). Penalties – Wittchow, Wat (boarding), 6:14; Blake Butzow, CR (cross checking), 13:39.

Shots on goal – Cedar Rapids 8-9-9 26. Waterloo 12-11-7 30.

Goalies – Cedar Rapids, Jake Hildebrand (12-8), Matt McNeely (17-14); Waterloo, Jay Williams (26-22).

Attendance – 3,500.

2012
Black Hawks 4, Cedar Rapids RoughRiders 3

Teddy bears weren't all that Zach Stepan brought to the ice on Thanksgiving night.

The 2012/13 Black Hawks were blessed with more offensive ability than any Waterloo team before them in the 21st century. Their goal-scoring acumen went beyond the forward line of Stepan, Taylor Cammarata, and Justin Kloos, but the trio did more than their share to help the Hawks record a club-record 273 goals that season. Stepan came to Waterloo after being selected by the Nashville Predators during the fourth round of the 2012 NHL Draft. Cammarata was named the USHL's Player of the Year and would be chosen by the New York Islanders in the third round the next summer. Kloos had been picked as Minnesota's Mr. Hockey award winner in 2012 and would make his NHL debut with the Minnesota Wild in 2017. By Thanksgiving, Kloos and Cammarata each had 25 points. Stepan had 21.

A two-week trip to Russia in August put the Hawks on a timeline ahead of the USHL's other clubs, leading to victories in 10 of their first 11 regular season games. Although the pace of wins slowed slightly in November, Waterloo's scoring did not. In their first 17 games, the Hawks scored three or more goals 15 times. A loss in Des Moines on the eve of the Thanksgiving game (6-5) resulted despite goals from Kloos, Stepan, and Cammarata. It was the third time Waterloo had been defeated during a game when they scored five goals or more.

After surrendering Des Moines' winning goal in the last three minutes, the Hawks saw the RoughRiders jump in front less than five minutes into the first period on Thanksgiving. Ian Brady's shot clanked off the post and sprang to Andrew Poturalski for a put back at 4:35. Waterloo's answer from Stepan resulted from a long shot three-and-a-half minutes later. It was Victor Newell's chance from the left point, which hit a RoughRider, went to the ice, sprang back up, and was tipped by the Nashville prospect over the shoulder of goalie Chad Catt.

Waterloo pulled ahead in the second at 4:41, with Stepan, Kloos, and Cammarata buzzing around the netmouth. Cammarata pulled the trigger from close range, with assists to both of his linemates. The Hawks made it 3-1 less than two minutes later as Stepan scored during a power play; after being tipped up, he regained his feet and knocked in a loose puck from the side of the net.

The RoughRiders slowed Waterloo's momentum with a power play score by Riley Bourbonnais at 9:13. However, Stepan reestablished the two-goal margin and completed his hat trick at 17:19, receiving a drop pass from Cammarata to put into an open side. It was the first hat trick by a Black Hawk on Thanksgiving since 1984.

Recording the first three-goal Thanksgiving performance by a Black Hawk in decades, Zach Stepan had everyone's attention at Young Arena. ©Stephanie Lyn Photography.

"The thing about tonight is, we didn't get many shots on net...but we were burying the chances we had," Stepan said after the game, also remarking, "I love playing with my line. Kloos and Cammarata have such good puck skills and find me so I had a couple of easy ones."

Scott Moldenhauer brought the RoughRiders to within a goal at 3:01 of the third, with a chance that deflected in off a defenseman. However, Waterloo's Cal Petersen stopped seven other attempts he saw during the period, and 21 for the game, to earn the win.

Cammarata (91), Kloos (87), and Stepan (78) ended the season as the

USHL's three leading point producers.

Cedar Rapids   1 1 1 – 3
Waterloo   1 3 0 – 4

First Period – 1, Cedar Rapids, Andrew Poturalski (Ian Brady, Corey Petrash), 4:35. 2, Waterloo, Zach Stepan (Vince Hinostroza, Victor Newell), 7:59. Penalties – Brandon Salerno, Wat (charging), 15:41.

Second Period – 3, Waterloo, Cammarata (Stepan, Justin Kloos), 4:41. 4, Waterloo, Stepan (Dane Cooper, Cammarata), 6:19 (pp). 5, Cedar Rapids, Riley Bourbonnais (Clay Anderson, Poturalski), 9:13 (pp). 6, Waterloo, Stepan (Cammarata, Charlie Manley), 17:19. Penalties – Bourbonnais, CR (tripping) 5:45; Gavin Bayreuther, CR (cross checking), 6:19; Stepan, Wat (cross checking), 7:38; Pijus Rulevicius, Wat (roughing), 11:52; Andrew Oglevie, CR (roughing), 11:52; Oglevie, CR (elbowing), 11:52.

Third Period – 7, Cedar Rapids, Scott Moldenhauer (Judd Peterson, Dylan Steman), 3:01. Penalties – Dylan Gareau, CR (diving), 7:57; Cooper, Wat (holding), 11:09.

Shots on goal – Cedar Rapids 9-7-8 24. Waterloo 6-7-5 18.

Goalies – Cedar Rapids, Chad Catt (18-14); Waterloo, Cal Petersen (24-21).

Attendance – 3,366.

2013
Black Hawks 3, Cedar Rapids RoughRiders 2

Before stepping onto the ice on November 28th, the RoughRiders had played the fewest games (16) of any USHL team during the 2013/14 season. The Black Hawks had skated on one more night and were tied with the Indiana Ice for the second-lowest game total. Only by dint of their limited opportunities to earn points, both Waterloo and Cedar Rapids were third in their respective conferences. The Hawks were 12-5-0, while the RoughRiders were one point better at 12-3-1 after a four-game winning streak.

Waterloo went to a power play almost immediately when Cedar Rapids defenseman Nathan Widman was cited for tripping during the first shift. The Hawks did not convert, but that would prove to be their lone special teams failure of the evening. However, the missed opportunity did later allow the RoughRiders to take and hold the lead for much of the opening period. Andrew Poturalski was below the left wing circle at 7:17 when his sharp-angled shot beat Cal Petersen. Cedar Rapids missed a chance to build on the lead when Patrick Russell was called for checking from behind at 11:40.

An additional offsetting double-minor for roughing with Cedar Rapids' Dylan Gareau kept Russell off the ice for most of what remained in the first period, but with 15.3 seconds left, Russell notched a goal to trigger the Teddy Bear Toss and level the score before intermission.

The teams exchanged goals again in the second, beginning when Cedar Rapids' Jack Rowe broke the tie, redirecting a centering pass by Judd Peterson at 6:46. However, Tyler Sheehy quickly evened the game, controlling a Zach Sanford rebound to score during a power play at 7:53.

Another power play made the difference in the third period. Waterloo pulled ahead for the first time at 3:14 when Hayden Shaw held in a clearing attempt and set up Peter Krieger for the go ahead score from the right wing circle. The Hawks killed off three subsequent Cedar Rapids power plays (finishing with a total of five successful kills) and fended off all ten RoughRider shots during the final frame.

Through the end of the 2019/20 hockey season, Patrick Russell is one of five 2013/14 Waterloo Black Hawks to have appeared in the National Hockey League. ©Stephanie Lyn Photography.

"It's not a situation we want...[to] kill off penalties like that," P.K. O'Handley remarked after the game, "but we were good and fortunate to do it, and I thought the power play was good, and it turned into special teams winning the game."

Cal Petersen earned the victory with 29 saves; Chris Birdsall was on the downside, despite making 38 stops.

Waterloo's power play would prove to be one of the team's defining components in 2013/14. The Hawks finished at the top of the league, converting more than 25 percent of their chances for the year. Scoring from special teams helped make Waterloo almost unbeatable during the middle months of the season. Beginning with a victory on the Saturday before Thanksgiving, the Black Hawks would earn at least one standings point in 23 consecutive games (21-0-2) through February 8th. With 44 wins that winter, Waterloo claimed the Anderson Cup while setting a new club record for victories in a season.

Cedar Rapids   1 1 0 – 2
Waterloo   1 1 1 – 3

First Period – 1, Cedar Rapids, Andrew Poturalski (Charlie Curti, Judd Peterson), 7:17. 2, Waterloo, Patrick Russell (Austin Vieth, Tyler Sheehy), 19:44. Penalties – Nathan Widman, CR (tripping), :17; Russell, Wat (checking from behind), 11:40; Russell, Wat (roughing double minor), 11:40; Dylan Gareau, CR (roughing double minor), 11:40; Zach Sanford, Wat (tripping), 14:42.

Second Period – 3, Cedar Rapids, Jack Rowe (J. Peterson, Ivan Provorov), 6:46. 4, Waterloo, Sheehy (Sanford, Mark Friedman), 7:53 (pp). Penalties – Nick Master, CR (hooking), 7:19.

Third Period – 5, Waterloo, Peter Krieger (Russell, Hayden Shaw), 3:14 (pp). Penalties – Mark Auk, CR (tripping), 2:08; Tyson McLellan, Wat (slashing), 5:10; Brandon Montour, Wat (slashing), 7:17; John Wiitala, Wat (tripping), 13:43.

Shots on goal – Cedar Rapids 9-12-10 31. Waterloo 13-17-11 41.

Goalies – Cedar Rapids, Chris Birdsall (41-38); Waterloo, Cal Petersen (31-29).

Attendance – 3,248.

2014
Cedar Rapids RoughRiders 4, Black Hawks 1

A Thanksgiving hockey game in Waterloo rarely represents an ending. For some casual fans, it's more likely to signify an unofficial beginning of the season, even though the Hawks play their first exhibitions in September. Even the weekend rarely ends on Thanksgiving night; typically one, and sometimes two, more games are lined up for the days which follow.

Yet the Thanksgiving game in 2014 was an inauspicious conclusion to Brandon Montour's brilliant career with the Black Hawks.

During a stunning 2013/14 campaign, Montour's status changed from that of an obscure, late-round USHL draft pick to a premier NHL Draft prospect. He finished among the league's top scorers and was named both Defenseman and Player of the Year. Waterloo won the 2013/14 Anderson Cup, then Montour led all players offensively during the Clark Cup Playoffs as the Hawks reached the championship series. In June, the Anaheim Ducks made him the 55th overall pick during the second round of the 2014 NHL Draft.

However, Montour's Canadian coursework from high school did not match the prerequisite criteria for the University of Massachusetts, and he returned to Waterloo in the fall to spend a semester arranging his academic affairs.

He continued to play well, ranking as the team's second-leading scorer through 16 games. Nevertheless, Montour's performance and the contributions of 2015 NHL Draft candidates Brock Boeser and Tom Novak couldn't lift the Hawks out of their bleak November. Waterloo entered the Thanksgiving meeting with Cedar Rapids on a seven-game losing streak, outscored during that time 39-16. The night before, they had been clobbered by Omaha, 10-4, falling to last place in the Western Conference.

The RoughRiders gave the Hawks little time to shake off their Wednesday night misery; Jiri Fronk was the beneficiary of fine passing and scored on a backhander from the slot 4:32 into the first period. Then Hugh McGing forced a turnover and completed an unassisted wraparound to make it 2-0 at 8:54.

Waterloo recovered momentarily five minutes later during a power play when Niko Hildenbrand redirected Montour's shot from the point. However, Matt O'Donnell reestablished a two-goal lead in quick succession, scoring from just above the right faceoff dot.

The second period was goalless, but the Hawks continued to pour on the shots. After a 14-5 lead in chances during the first, Waterloo followed up with an 18-8 edge in opportunities during the second. RoughRider goaltender Ben Blacker stopped everything after Hildenbrand's tip-in and went to the locker room at the second intermission with 31 saves.

Cedar Rapids clamped down in the third, limiting Waterloo to five shots on frame. The only scoring during the period came on an empty-netter with 14.8 seconds left. The result ended Waterloo's six-year streak of wins during the holiday game. The streak of more immediate concern – the now-eight-game losing streak – stretched to ten before the Hawks claimed a win in Fargo during the first weekend of December. Between that night and Waterloo's next Thanksgiving win, Montour would start and end a brief NCAA career, become an American Hockey League All-Star, and be on the cusp of a call-up to Anaheim for his NHL debut.

Brandon Montour celebrates one of the 83 points he recorded in 77 USHL regular season games. He also had 16 points in 12 playoff contests for the Black Hawks. ©Stephanie Lyn Photography.

Cedar Rapids   3 0 1 – 4
Waterloo   1 0 0 – 1

First Period – 1, Cedar Rapids, Jiri Fronk (Mitch Reinke, Erik Foley), 4:32. 2, Cedar Rapids, Hugh McGing (unassisted), 8:54. 3, Waterloo, Niko Hildenbrand (Brandon Montour, Tom Novak), 13:52 (pp). 4, Cedar Rapids, Matt O'Donnall (Fronk), 15:06. Penalties – Andrew Oglevie, CR (hooking), 12:56.

Second Period – no scoring. Penalties – Hildenbrand, Wat (hooking), 8:26; O'Donnell, CR (slashing), 11:33; O'Donnell, CR (roughing), 17:26.

Third Period – 5, Cedar Rapids, Andrew Gaus (Logan Von Ruden, Oglevie), 19:45 (en). Penalties – Marcel Godbout, Wat (high sticking double minor), 13:34.

Shots on goal – Cedar Rapids 5-7-11 23. Waterloo 14-18-5 37.

Goalies – Cedar Rapids, Ben Blacker (37-36); Waterloo, Hayden Lavigne (5-2), Kris Carlson (17-17).

Attendance – 2,934.

2015
Cedar Rapids RoughRiders 5, Black Hawks 1

Ben Blacker returned looking for a Thanksgiving encore. The Black Hawks hoped for a much different sort of repeat performance in net during the holiday game.

When the 2015/16 season began, both clubs expected to count on veteran goaltenders: Blacker for Cedar Rapids, and Cale Morris for Waterloo. Blacker was steady through the first two months of the season, riding mid-pack among the USHL's goalies while his team held a similar position in the league standings. Morris started well for the Hawks, playing in nearly every game and delivering a goals-against average just over 2.00. However, when the Hawks and RoughRiders met for the first time on Thanksgiving night, it wasn't Blacker-vs.-Morris.

Two weeks earlier, during the third period of a game versus the Lincoln Stars, Morris had injured his groin. He would be out of the lineup until the end of December. Days before that Lincoln game, backup goalie Dayton Rasmussen had asked for a trade, unhappy with his playing time.

Unheralded Drew Hotte arrived in Waterloo's moment of need. Hotte had been with the Black Hawks during the exhibition schedule and was quickly reacquired from the North American Hockey League after Rasmussen's departure. The Morris injury led to Hotte's debut, cold off the bench, but he helped Waterloo hang on for a win. During a start the next weekend against the Des Moines Buccaneers, Hotte delivered a shutout. At Thanksgiving, his numbers compared favorably to Morris. Most importantly, he had given Waterloo a chance to win each game. Unfortunately, Hotte had little opportunity to be the hero when the RoughRiders visited.

In the first period, Cedar Rapids capitalized on a couple of Waterloo miscues. Near the nine minute mark, two Hawks collided, and that set up Ross

Colton to lift a shot through traffic and under the crossbar. Not quite ten minutes later at 18:36, Waterloo worked the puck free deep in their own zone but could not get it out. Hotte had no chance to stop Sam Sternschein's goal from pointblank range, on a play created behind the net by Liam Walsh.

Ben Blacker was at the bottom of the Black Hawks' troubles in back-to-back Thanksgiving games He stopped all but two of 67 shots he faced during the holiday matchup in consecutive years. ©Stephanie Lyn Photography.

Waterloo's apparent break came with just under three minutes left in the second. Nick Swaney recorded the lone Waterloo goal, following a puck to the net and flipping it home after Ronnie Hein's initial chance popped out of Blacker's glove.

Colton answered back 17 seconds later, firing a shot that eluded Hotte from the left corner.

"We started off kind of slow. After we got down 2-0 it was hard to get rolling, and then we got the goal," Hein observed after the game. "But then they sucked the life out of us with that third goal. It seemed like everybody gave up."

The RoughRiders added another with six seconds left before intermission as Justin Cole redirected a power play chance. John DeRoche capped the scoring 1:54 into the third with an opportunity from close range.

Waterloo outshot Cedar Rapids 30-23, but Blacker made 29 saves for his second Thanksgiving victory. He became the first visiting goalie to win twice on Thanksgiving since Bobby Goepfert in 2000 and 2001.

Cedar Rapids	2 2 1	– 5
Waterloo	0 1 0	– 1

First Period – 1, Cedar Rapids, Ross Colton (John Snodgrass), 8:57. 2, Cedar Rapids, Sam Sternschein (Liam Walsh, Jack Ahcan), 18:36. Penalties – Michael Davies, Wat (hooking), 5:15.

Second Period – 3, Waterloo, Nick Swaney (Ronnie Hein, Liam Pecararo), 17:11. 4, Cedar Rapids, Colton (Hugh McGing, David Nemecek), 17:28. 5, Cedar Rapids, Justin Cole (Mitch Reinke, Taylor Brierley), 19:54 (pp). Penalties – Zac Robbins, CR (roughing), 3:21; Pecararo, Wat (roughing), 3:21; Brandon Schultz, Wat (kneeing), 3:21; Colton, CR (kneeing), 12:30; Sternschein, CR (roughing), 19:07; Sam Rossini, Wat (roughing), 19:07; Alex Robert, Wat (cross checking), 19:19.

Third Period – 6, Cedar Rapids, Johnny DeRoche (Cal Burke, Matt Filipe), 1:54. Penalties – Ben Foley, CR (roughing), 2:28; Schultz, Wat (slashing), 4:34.

Shots on Goal – Cedar Rapids 8-6-9 23. Waterloo 10-12-8 30.

Goalies – Cedar Rapids, Ben Blacker (30-29); Waterloo, Drew Hotte (23-18).

Attendance – 2,907.

2016
Black Hawks 1, Cedar Rapids RoughRiders 0

The Cedar Rapids RoughRiders had never come to Young Arena in circumstances like what they faced in November of 2016. The previous spring, Mark Carlson's team had been the only USHL club with 40 wins. They had clinched the Anderson Cup in Waterloo with one game to spare during the 2015/16 schedule. Seven months later, they returned for the first time with their fortunes completely altered; the RoughRiders were 0-15-2 to start the new season.

Unsurprisingly, no team had allowed more goals or scored less. Through 17 games there wasn't a Cedar Rapids player with more than seven points. Sixteen-year-old goaltender Drew DeRidder had taken the starting job and performed better than the older, more experienced players the RoughRiders tried. On Thanksgiving, DeRidder nearly surprised the Hawks for his first USHL win.

At the other end of the age spectrum and in the opposing net, Robbie Beydoun had come to Waterloo after two seasons with the Fargo Force. Caught in a crunch with too many players born in 1996, Fargo dealt him to the Hawks before the season began. The day before Beydoun turned 20, he made 27 saves against his former team for a 2-0 shutout during his Waterloo debut. He whitewashed two more opponents and had a goals-against average at 1.91 when Thanksgiving arrived.

Waterloo kept DeRidder under nearly constant pressure during the first period. The Hawks lobbed 17 shots his direction to no effect. The moment which did excite the home fans came five minutes before intermission. Rookie forward Jack Drury circled up with Cedar Rapids' Dalton Messina for a scrap near the RoughRider bench. The Waterloo 16-year-old held his own in the encounter with an opponent who would finish among the league's penalty minute leaders. In the changing atmosphere of the early 21st century, the altercation was a rarity; there hadn't been a fight during the Thanksgiving game since 2007.

The second period passed with no goals and no penalties. Waterloo continued to hold the balance of opportunities, outshooting Cedar Rapids 30-9 through 40 minutes. Nonetheless, the game was still scoreless. Facing a winless archrival for a traditional holiday game in front of the largest crowd of the season to that point (2,920), tension was mounting for the Hawks.

Robbie Beydoun was ready for everything Cedar Rapids sent his direction, and the Hawks needed every save. ©Stephanie Lyn Photography.

Three minutes into the third period, the matchup broke Waterloo's way. Emil Ohrvall had been out of the lineup for four games with a shoulder injury, but at that moment, he was in the right spot to gather the puck as the trailing forward coming into the Cedar Rapids zone. Taking aim from the left circle and using a RoughRider defenseman to screen DeRidder, Ohrvall lifted the puck diagonally to the opposite top corner.

"It gave our bench extreme life," said Black Hawks Head Coach P.K. O'Handley, "Human nature sets in, and [you say] 'are we going to score here?' I think the players knew we were playing well, just 'are we going to score?' Once that happened, I thought we loosened up a bit."

Neither side earned many more chances, with a combined total of just nine shots in the third. Beydoun picked up his fourth shutout of the season making only 14 saves. The game surpassed three other low-scoring Thanksgivings which had ended 2-1 (two of those were 1-1 at the end of regulation).

The RoughRiders would earn their first win of the season at the Black Hawks' expense, 3-0 in Cedar Rapids two nights later.

Cedar Rapids   0 0 0 – 0
Waterloo   0 0 1 – 1

First Period – no scoring. Penalties – Jack Drury, Wat (tripping), 1:58; Dalton Messina, CR (fighting), 15:02; Messina, CR (misconduct), 15:02; Drury, Wat (fighting), 15:02; Drury, Wat (misconduct), 15:02; Ben Foley, CR (hooking), 16:37.

Second Period – no scoring. Penalties – none.

Third Period – 1, Waterloo, Emil Ohrvall (Logan Jenuwine, Ace Cowans), 3:13. Penalties – Riese Zmolek, CR (roughing), 9:11; Garrett Wait, Wat (roughing), 9:11; Jake Ryczek, Wat (hooking), 10:55.

Shots on Goal – Cedar Rapids 4-5-5 14. Waterloo 17-13-4 34.

Goalies – Cedar Rapids, Drew DeRidder (34-33); Waterloo, Robbie Beydoun (14-14).

Attendance – 2,920.

2017
Black Hawks 5, Cedar Rapids RoughRiders 2

If Marek Valach had scored five seconds sooner, it might have been a much different game. Late in the first period, the RoughRiders went to a power play when Solag Bakich was called for slashing. Waterloo's Kyle Koopman followed him to the penalty box for the same infraction with only moments remaining before intermission. Cedar Rapids started the second with 17 seconds of five-on-three power play time. Valach's goal broke a scoreless tie at the 21-second mark (four seconds after Bakich had come back onto the ice) putting the teams back at even strength.

Had the RoughRiders capitalized during their two-man advantage and remained on the power play, it's hard to see how the game's decisive second period would have followed the same course.

Whatever momentum the visitors achieved from the early power play was quickly overcome. A fast passing sequence in transition sent the puck from Jack Drury to Bobby Trivigno to Garrett Wait in quick succession. The third-year veteran's shot from the left circle hit the net to even the score at 1:54.

Seconds later, a spate of penalties sent the Hawks shorthanded for the third time in the game. Drury was on the ice for the next faceoff, and shortly after play restarted, the noted penalty-killer was speeding up the rink on a shorthanded breakaway. Drury was unable to finish the chance when he was upended by a back-checking defender, so instead, he was awarded a penalty shot.

Waterloo had completed the first quarter of their schedule the night before and owned one shorthanded goal in that time. Individually, Drury had one goal from the first 15 games as well, but the penalty shot doubled both totals. The Harvard recruit cut from right to left, starting from the circle, moving across the slot, and then beating Blake Pietila with a low shot between the pads. By the end of the season, the Hawks would accumulate a USHL-leading 16 shorthanded goals (Drury would finish with five). Drury went on to score with increasing regularity in a 24-goal campaign, which led the Carolina Hurricanes to pick him in the second round of the 2018 NHL Draft.

Jack Drury on a breakaway, just a moment before he was pulled down, leading to a penalty shot. ©Stephanie Lyn Photography.

"I think everyone was a little nervous for the Thanksgiving Day game, it's a big game," Drury said. "But it was good to see us get it done in the second period and push from there."

Waterloo maintained the lead through a fourth Cedar Rapids power play in the middle of the period, then pulled away. Five minutes before intermission, Ethan Johnson forced a turnover at center; his shot was blocked but came to Matej Blumel at the top of the crease. Blumel knocked the puck across the goal line to make the score 3-1. Then on the first Waterloo power play of the night, the Hawks added another tally on Drury's redirection of a Jackson Cates attempt from the right dot.

In the third, the Hawks built their lead to its largest margin at 7:28 when Cates pulled the puck out of a net-front scramble and fired it into an open side. The 5-1 score held until the final three minutes, but the RoughRiders could only trim Waterloo's lead to three. The Hawks held them to seven shots in the final period and 22 for the night.

Cedar Rapids   0 1 1 – 2
Waterloo   0 4 1 – 5

First Period – no scoring. Penalties – Solag Bakich, Wat (slashing), 18:17; Kyle Koopman, Wat (slashing), 19:42.

Second Period – 1, Cedar Rapids, Marek Valach (Nathan Smith, Harrison Roy), :21 (pp). 2, Waterloo, Garrett Wait (Bobby Trivigno, Jack Drury), 1:54. 3, Waterloo, Drury (penalty shot), 2:27 (sh). 4, Waterloo, Matej Blumel (Ethan Johnson), 15:04. 5, Waterloo, Drury (Jackson Cates, Hank Sorensen), 16:51 (pp). Penalties – Will Zmolek, CR (roughing), 2:13; Bakich, Wat (roughing), 2:13; Ben Copeland, Wat (tripping), 2:13; Danny DiGrande, Wat (tripping), 10:19; Kyle Looft, CR (tripping), 16:18.

Third Period – 6, Waterloo, Cates (Copeland, Bakich), 7:28. 7, Cedar Rapids, Kevin Lombardi (Ilya Sushko, Zmolek), 16:58. Penalties – Drury, Wat (high sticking), 3:09; Jordan Timmons, CR (roughing double minor), 5:27; Mason Palmer, Wat (roughing double minor), 5:27; Lombardi, CR (checking from behind), 13:21.

Shots on Goal – Cedar Rapids 9-6-7 22. Waterloo 5-15-9 29.

Goalies – Cedar Rapids, Blake Pietila (29-24). Waterloo, Jared Moe (22-20).

Attendance – 2,962.

2018
Black Hawks 4, Cedar Rapids RoughRiders 1

On November 7th, the Black Hawks traded veteran Michael Ferrandino to the Central Illinois Flying Aces for Brehdan Engum. It was the beginning of Engum's first full USHL season after he had appeared in a dozen games for the Bloomington-based team the year before. The defenseman quickly recognized the change in atmosphere and expectations.

"It was a lot more demanding, and there was a lot more set culture for the team. In Central Illinois, it wasn't quite the same," Engum noted, further expanding the comparison, "Here, the coaches know exactly what they want out of their players, and that translates to the locker room too, and the guys know what they need to put out there every night."

The Hawks hoped the 6-foot-2-inch Engum would add some heft to the blue line without sacrificing mobility for size. Offense from the Burnsville, Minnesota, native would be a bonus; Engum did not have a USHL point at the time of the trade.

Just over two weeks later, neither the Black Hawks nor the RoughRiders had scored during the first period on Thanksgiving. An apparent goal for the visitors was disallowed because Hawks goaltender Logan Stein had been knocked out of position. Although Cedar Rapids later skated with the period's only power play, Waterloo limited them to six total shots, and the Hawks carried play for much of the first 20 minutes.

Almost three minutes into the second, Engum and Waterloo celebrated a breakthrough. Hank Sorensen – who had played against Engum in the Minnesota High School State Tournament during the spring of 2016 – swept a pass across the high slot. Just a couple of steps inside the blue line at the left point, Engum fired a wrister which flew to the top corner.

"It was 20-some games," Engum said later, admitting that not recording a point was something which had been on his mind, but adding, "I take pride in being a solid defensive player, so points have never been the biggest issue to me, but it was nice to get that first one out of the way."

The scoreboard over Brehdan Engum's shoulder indicates this photo was captured just a moment before his first USHL goal. ©Stephanie Lyn Photography.

Waterloo built the lead late in the period. The scoring at that point came from the top of the stat sheet. Perhaps no Black Hawks team has had more European offensive flair than the one on the ice that fall. Czech-born Matej Blumel started the Thanksgiving game fourth in league scoring with 24 points. Russian forward Vladislav Firstov was not far behind with 19 and among the leading rookies. Swedish veteran Emil Ohrvall had a dozen goals, tied with Blumel for third in the USHL.

At 14:56, Ohrvall followed his own errant shot behind the net; from that position, he connected with Blumel, whose attempt beat Blake Pietila while the Cedar Rapids goalie was screened by a defender. Firstov added one more at 17:17, looping from the right circle to the slot to lift a wrist shot past Pietila's stick. Firstov recorded a second goal just over a minute into the third period to make the score 4-0.

The RoughRiders recorded their lone goal with six minutes remaining. It was one of just four Cedar Rapids shots in the third period and 14 for the game. Waterloo did not hold an opponent to fewer shots all season. Appropriately Engum – the defensive defenseman who scored his first goal – was named the night's number one star.

Cedar Rapids   0   0   1 – 1
Waterloo   0   3   1 – 4

First Period – no scoring. Penalties – Brock Paul, Wat (tripping), 15:07.

Second Period – 1, Waterloo, Brehdan Engum (Hank Sorensen, Joe Cassetti), 2:57. 2, Waterloo, Matej Blumel (Emil Ohrvall, Matt Cameron), 14:56. 3, Waterloo, Vladislav Firstov (Wyatt Schingoethe, Cassetti), 17:17. Penalties – Mason Palmer, Wat (tripping), 18:26.

Third Period – 4, Waterloo, Firstov (Ethan Szmagaj, Emil Ohrvall), 1:09. 5, Cedar Rapids, Jordan Tonelli (Will Zmolek, Max Sasson), 14:00. Penalties – Nathan Smith, CR (slashing), 15:26.

Shots on Goal – Cedar Rapids 6-4-4 14. Waterloo 15-15-14 44.

Goalies – Cedar Rapids, Blake Pietila (44-40); Waterloo, Logan Stein (14-13).

Attendance – 3,159.

2019
Black Hawks 4, Cedar Rapids RoughRiders 0

A wealth of veteran players helped Waterloo slingshot into the 2019/20 schedule. The Black Hawks drew on experience to win their first seven games, a season-opening record for the club. All but two of those victories were in close games (settled by two goals or less). The poise of second- and third-year players helped make the difference and immediately moved Waterloo to the top of the USHL Western Conference. The Hawks had a four-point hold on first place by Thanksgiving.

The starting lineups which were announced in the minutes before the holiday game featured a contingent of veterans for both teams. All six forwards had been on the ice for the traditional matchup a year earlier. Each side had one returning defenseman out for the opening draw. Logan Stein leaned in to watch the faceoff from the Black Hawks' crease for the second consecutive year.

"I think I've improved my awareness and knowing what's going to happen," Stein said, reflecting about his second year of junior competition, "I feel like I'm one step ahead, and I also feel like my positioning has gotten a lot better and my preparation for games has gotten a lot better."

He entered the action on that Thursday night as the USHL's leading goalie, measured by both goals-against average and save percentage.

The Hawks gave their netminder a lead to protect 4:32 into the first period. Xander Lamppa was waiting between the left wing circle and the top of the crease and deflected Jacob Bengtsson's low shot to the opposite top corner of the net. Following a stoppage for the annual Teddy Bear Toss, Waterloo went to a power play a couple of shifts later when the RoughRiders were caught with too many men on the ice. Another chance originating from the left point led to a special teams conversion. Ethan Szmagaj's try came off the end wall, and Connor Caponi kicked it to the top of the crease. That's where Kyle Haskins pounced to lift a backhander under the crossbar.

Two second period goals pushed the score to 4-0. At 5:56, Bengtsson didn't get all of a shot from the top of the right circle, but it still provided his second point of the night. The fluttering chance went over the shoulder of Derek Mullahy to build the lead. Then during a power play with less than five minutes left before intermission, Griffin Ness slung a pass from the side of the net to Ryder Rolston in the left circle. Rolston put the puck between the pipes before Mullahy could move from post-to-post. It was the only point recorded during the game by a player who hadn't been a Black Hawk in 2018/19.

Through 40 minutes, Waterloo had outshot Cedar Rapids 25-15. Stein preserved his perfect night with 13 third period saves, making him only the fourth Waterloo goalie to earn a Thanksgiving shutout. He also became the first Black Hawks netminder since Cal Petersen to win the holiday game in consecutive years. Two nights later in Cedar Rapids, Stein stopped 27 more RoughRider shots for a 1-0 win. The two shutouts were half of his league-leading total of four during the 2019/20 season.

A little traffic near the front of the net was no problem for Logan Stein in the first of two Thanksgiving weekend shutouts. ©Stephanie Lyn Photography.

Cedar Rapids   0 0 0 – 0
Waterloo   2 2 0 – 4

First Period – 1, Waterloo, Xander Lamppa (Jacob Bengtsson, Ethan

Szmagaj), 4:32. 2, Waterloo, Kyle Haskins (Connor Caponi, Szmagaj), 7:46 (pp). Penalties – bench minor, CR (too many men), 6:16.

Second Period – 3, Waterloo, Bengtsson (Haskins, Wyatt Schingoethe), 5:56. 4, Waterloo, Ryder Rolston (Lamppa, Griffin Ness), 15:02 (pp). Penalties – Mason Reiners, Wat (roughing), 7:33; Darian Gotz, CR (tripping), 14:09; Matthew Argentina, Wat (slashing), 16:55.

Third Period – no scoring. Penalties – Schingoethe, Wat (slashing), 6:42.

Shots on Goal – Cedar Rapids 7-8-13 28. Waterloo 12-13-10 35.

Goalies – Cedar Rapids, Shamil Shmakov (12-10), Derek Mullahy (23-21); Waterloo, Logan Stein (28-28).

Attendance – 3,064.

ACKNOWLEDGEMENTS

This retrospective look at Waterloo Black Hawks Thanksgiving games would not have been possible without help from a wide variety of people. First and foremost, my wife Laura provided patience and calming assistance as the project stretched longer and took different turns than expected (all such projects do in one way or another, and this one was no exception).

I am also always grateful to the staff at the Waterloo Public Library for their role in preserving local history. The writers and photographers of the *Waterloo Courier* provided much of the source material which makes it possible to give Thanksgivings of the past a new life, and the library is a wonderful repository of that history.

With a professional tendency toward words (spoken or written), pictures have never been an area of much ease for me, so I would like to thank the following people for their various assistance with the images in this book: Meta Hemenway-Forbes of the *Courier*, Steph Regenold of Stephanie Lyn Photography, Charlie Larson and Aaron Sims of the Milwaukee Admirals, Bob Batcheller, George Griffiths, Sarah D'Antonio-Gard of the Robert and Elizabeth Dole Archive and Special Collections at the Robert J. Dole Institute of Politics/University of Kansas, Kristy McNeil at the University of Michigan, Brad Leeper of INVISION Architecture, Mike Brown, and Brandon McConnell.

Also thanks to many Black Hawks fans, who over the years have contributed old programs and documents to the team's informal organizational library. By saving these items, and with your willingness to donate them, you have helped the team know a great deal more about its history than would otherwise be possible.

Finally, thanks to all Black Hawks fans for making Thanksgiving an enduring part of the team's tradition. It is something for which to be thankful, far outside the last days of November.

INDEX OF WATERLOO'S THANKSGIVING GOAL-SCORERS

Anderson, Tim - 1975 (2)
Arhontas, Matt - 2005
Arnold, Derek - 2008
Arrigoni, Todd - 1980 (2)
Banaszek, Jim - 1980 (2)
Barnes, Tyler - 2009
Barzee, Jack - 1967 (2), 1973 (2)
Batley, Chris - 1966
Bengtsson, Jacob - 2019
Bennett, Bill - 1974
Bissett, Tom - 1984
Blom, Stan - 1976, 1978
Blumel, Matej - 2017, 2018
Borisenok, Mike - 2005
Boxer, Jay - 1987
Brouk, Adam - 1992
Brown, Charlie - 1973 (2)
Brown, Chris - 1988
Cameranesi, Tony - 2011 (2)
Cammarata, Taylor - 2011, 2012
Canady, Brian - 1998, 2000
Carlson, Ross - 2002
Cates, Jackson - 2017
Chandler, Matt - 1997

Chernoff, Mike (Iowa Stars) - 1969 (2)
Christianson, Todd - 1982 (2)
Clubbe, Rick - 1977
Coakley, Chris - 1993
Cook, Brian - 1986
Dagenais, Mike - 2002
Detloff, Steve - 1984
Dietz, Doug - 1982
Divjak, Patrick - 2009 (2)
Dolan, Scott - 1984
Drury, Jack - 2017 (2)
Engum, Brehdan - 2018
Falls, Doug - 1975
Finnerty, Chris - 1970
Finseth, Cale - 1998
Firstov, Vladislav - 2018 (2)
Folden, Brian - 1993
Fulghum, Luke - 1998
Giannetti, Mark - 1994
Gospodar, Jim - 1975
Griffiths, George - 1983, 1984 (3)
Grubb, John - 1998, 1999
Grum, Bill - 1979
Hale, Ryan - 1997

Hansen, James - 2011
Haskins, Kyle - 2019
Hayes, Eriah - 2008
Hildenbrand, Niko - 2014
Hill, Jamie - 2010
Hinostroza, Vince - 2011
Hosken, Keith - 1981
Hughes, Gunnar - 2010
Iwaskiewicz, Phil - 1974
Johnson, Brad - 1989
Johnson, Paul - 1966, 1967 (5), 1970
Juutilainen, Jan-Mikael - 2006 (2)
Karabelinkoff, Dan - 1983
Kempffer, Mick - 1988
Kenny, Rob - 1987
Kessel, Blake - 2007
Kessler, Chuck - 1978
Kimball, Dan - 1982 (2)
King, Kim - 1976
Kleven, Chris - 1985
Klostreich, Page - 1987
Knaeble, Brian - 1999
Krieger, Peter - 2013
Krohn, Rod - 1979
Lampman, Todd - 1970
Lamppa, Xander - 2019
Larson, Nick - 2008
Laurila, Marty - 1993
Leier, Mike - 1989
Leskun, Butch - 1964
Lesyshen, John - 1970, 1973, 1974 (2)
MacDonald, Scott - 2011
Machowski, Tom - 1978 (2)
Markham, Ryan - 2000
Matlock, Bryan - 1972
Mazur, Dave - 1966
McCoshen, Ian - 2011
McGregor, Cam - 1977 (2)
McKechnie, Walt (Iowa Stars) - 1969

McRae, Bud - 1966
Middleton, Kent - 1983
Milardo, Ron - 1978
Miller, Ben - 2008
Montpetit, Brock - 2009 (2)
Motzko, Bob - 1979
Murphy, Hal - 1972, 1973
Nagurski, Ron - 1973
Noonan, Kevin - 1983 (2)
Notermann, Mike - 1985 (2)
Ogee, Tom - 1997
Ohrvall, Emil - 2016
O'Leary, Bob - 1970
Oleson, Chris - 1989
Olson, R.J. - 1987
Orban, Bill (Iowa Stars) - 1969
Papa, Ryan - 2010
Paul, Doug - 1966
Pavelski, Joe - 2002, 2003
Pennock, Dale - 1973
Rafferty, Pat - 1987
Redmond, Dick (Iowa Stars) - 1969
Regan, Jeff - 1979 (2)
Rehkamp, Joe - 2011
Rodrigue, Jacques - 1975
Rolston, Ryder - 2019
Rooney, Bill - 1986
Rose, Jon - 1987
Ruelle, Emery - 1964 (4), 1966
Russell, Patrick - 2013
Ryan, Mitch - 2005
Samuels-Thomas, Jordan - 2008
Sauer, E.J. - 1984 (2)
Scheid, Chris - 1985 (2), 1986
Schuster, Jacob - 2005
Seidel, John - 1977
Sheehy, Tyler - 2013
Skime, Larry - 1972
Sommer, Roy - 1977
Sova, Dan - 2009
Starkey, Ed - 1975, 1977 (3)

Steinmetz, Todd - 1992, 1994
Stepan, Zach - 2012 (3)
Stephens, B.J. - 1997
Swaney, Nick - 2015
Swick, Dave - 1970
Taylor, Hobie - 1975
Taylor, Rod - 1983 (2), 1984 (3)
Taylor, Tim - 1967
Testwuide, J.P. - 2003
Testwuide, Mike - 2005
Thompson, Todd - 1982
Trudeau, Roger - 1994
Turcotte, Todd - 1989
Tyler, Jim - 1984 (3)
Vesel, Jesse - 2004
Wait, Garrett - 2017
Wehr, Brian - 1988, 1989
Whitmore, Derek - 2002
Wolfe, Trevor - 2000
Wormith, Paul - 1974
Yackel, Ken - 1977 (2)

www.ingramcontent.com/pod-product-compliance
Lightning Source LLC
Chambersburg PA
CBHW062013180426
43199CB00035B/2641